BRICK PROJECTS
FOR THE LANDSCAPE

BRICK PROJECTS
FOR THE LANDSCAPE
16 easy-to-build designs

ALAN & GILL BRIDGEWATER

CREATIVE
PUBLISHING
international

CHANHASSEN, MINNESOTA
www.creativepub.com

First published in 2004 in the USA and Canada by
Creative Publishing international, Inc.

18705 Lake Drive East
Chanhassen
Minnesota 55317
1-800-328-3895
www.creativepub.com

President/CEO: Michael Eleftheriou
Vice President/Publisher: Linda Ball
Vice President of Sales & Marketing: Kevin Haas
Executive Editor: Bryan Trandem

Published in United Kingdom by New Holland Publishers (UK) Ltd

ISBN 1-58923-187-2

Editorial Direction: Rosemary Wilkinson
Senior Editor: Clare Sayer
Production: Hazel Kirkman

Designed and created for New Holland by AG&G BOOKS
Designer: Glyn Bridgewater
Illustrators: Gill Bridgewater and Coral Mula
Project design: Alan and Gill Bridgewater
Photography: AG&G Books and Ian Parsons
Editor: Fiona Corbridge
Brickwork: Alan Bridgewater

Reproduction by Pica Digital, Singapore
Printed and bound in Malaysia by Times Offset (M) Sdn. Bhd.

Contents

Part 1: Techniques 8

Part 2: Projects 32

Introduction

When we saw our first house—an isolated Victorian farmhouse—we were confronted with numerous redbrick outbuildings that were all, to some degree, tumbledown ruins. However, the bricks were crisp and hard-edged, and the lime mortar soft—so much so that we were able to scrape the bricks clean. We decided to salvage bricks from the outbuildings to renovate and extend the main house. We made contact with a retired master bricklayer in the village, who was prepared to give advice.

We spent the next ten years working on our home—Gill scraping the bricks, and our two toddler sons doing their bit. Of course, it was hard work, and we made lots of mistakes, but we were spurred on by the excitement of it all. We had the time of our lives, building everything from walls and arches through to pillars, posts, raised beds, paths, sheds, and even the top half of a well!

The ambition of this book is to share with you all the pleasures of working with brick to create garden features. With each project, we take you through the procedures of considering the design and working out how it might be modified to suit your individual needs. We tell you how to use the tools and materials, and explain the

essential techniques. Illustrations and photographs show how best to achieve the step-by-step procedures; in fact, we take you through all the stages of designing, making, constructing, and finishing.

Brickwork doesn't require complex tools or specialized knowledge: it is about working with your hands in the garden, and the pleasure of using your mind and body to create exciting structures.

Best of luck!

Alan & Gill

HEALTH AND SAFETY

Some of the procedures for making the brickwork projects are hazardous, so before starting work, read the advice below:

- Some projects are physically demanding: if you have doubts about whether you are up to it, get advice from your physician. When lifting heavy items, minimize back strain by holding the item close to your body, and bend your knees rather than your back.
- Never operate a machine, or attempt a difficult lifting or maneuvering task, if you are feeling tired.
- Wear gloves and goggles when you are handling and breaking hardpan. Wear gloves, goggles, and a dust-mask when mixing cement, using a circular saw with masonry blade, or cutting bricks with a hammer and chisel.
- Follow manufacturers' directions when using tools and materials.
- Keep a first-aid kit and telephone nearby, in case of an emergency and, if possible, avoid working alone.
- Do not build a pond if you have young children. Other water features are safer, but even so, never leave children unsupervised.
- Use a safety electricity circuit breaker (between the power socket and the plug) when operating power tools and water pumps, to prevent electric shock.

Part I: Techniques

Design and planning

The art of working with bricks relies on the coordination between mind, hand, and eye: the key words are planning, rhythm, repetition, and timing. The trick is to fit the components together with the minimum of measuring and as few cuts as possible. If you do have to make a cut, the challenge is to get it right the first time! If you can use the bricks as you find them—new, salvaged, seconds, or left over from another job—so much the better.

FIRST CONSIDERATIONS

• What do you want to achieve? Write down the aspects that are important to you, and look at magazines, books, and other people's gardens to assess the possibilities. If necessary, change our project designs to suit your needs.

• Bricks are made in many colors and textures. Do some research into what is available, and see what appeals.

• To make a project fit better into your space, you may have to consider changing its size, shape, and proportions. Would it, for example, look better as a larger but low, long, and thin structure, or as a square rather than round structure? Use the dimensions of a brick to dictate the precise overall project dimensions—working in a number of whole bricks wherever possible. (See pages 24–25 for how to cut bricks.)

• Location and orientation are important. Mark the envisaged position with sticks, plastic sheet, or plywood, and look out for possible problems such as the blocking of routes through the garden, unfortunate viewpoints, and the casting of shadows.

• If the project is a pond or water feature, does it require a long trench to be dug in the garden to bury a power cable, and is this possible?

• Are there parts of a project's construction that you don't understand? Try working out the problem on paper or mocking up the structure with real materials.

• Calculate the costs and time involved, to make sure that the project is feasible.

Choosing a suitable project

Sometimes it is easy to get carried away and build something massive that dominates the space and, quite frankly, looks out of place because the scale is wrong and the style is not suitable. So before you decide what to build, take stock of your garden or yard and consider how to improve it. If it is cluttered, you may want to rebuild an existing feature to make it smaller, stronger, or more decorative. If the area is wasteland or a blank canvas, design the whole garden first; when you are ready to build brickwork projects, make sure they fit into the overall scheme.

Garden features are more than basic structures that are constructed out of necessity—they are also decorative. You may need to change the appearance or style of a project to suit your garden. For example, a simple, well-proportioned brick planter would suit a modern scheme, but for a Victorian garden, it would be more appropriate to incorporate detailing and decoration. From a safety point of view, avoid building ponds and some water features if you have young children.

Planning the project

The first part of a project (and one of the most important) is deciding on its precise size and location. For a patio outside your back door, for example, you need to know its finished height, how it slopes in order to drain rainwater away from the house, and its exact size to the nearest brick and mortar joint.

In the projects in this book, a lot of the planning has been done for you, but do take note of any advice or exceptions that suggest you might need to revise the design, and which refer you to a page within this techniques section. Do a survey of the site and draw simple scaled diagrams on graph paper, showing how the footing is constructed and how the project is built. Some structures pose more obvious planning problems: steps, for example, have to conform to certain dimensions otherwise you will trip over them; walls that are too high or long can lean or fall down without the benefit of extra support (see pages 29–30).

Every brickwork project requires a footing: a firm, level (or sometimes slightly sloping, in the case of a patio) base on which to build, otherwise it will collapse. It is very important to use an appropriate footing, and to plan it in a drawing to show its size and depth. For example, if you want a patio to be level with the surrounding ground, the patio needs to take into account the thickness of the bricks that will be used for paving.

Buying the right tools and materials

Once you have sorted out the project design in detail, you can assess what you need to build it. Sometimes, it is necessary to compromise with both tools and materials in order to make a project affordable. If that is the case, ensure you have enough time to do the work with basic manual tools, and don't resort to inferior materials that will deteriorate quickly.

If you haven't got a wonderful set of tools, consider borrowing or hiring better ones. A cement mixer is worth hiring if you are working on a large project, unless you enjoy body-building exercise! Call around for quotes for materials, and order in bulk when possible. The choice of bricks available depends on your locality; you can also consider using second-quality bricks (rejects) or reclaimed (secondhand) bricks.

BRICKWORK DESIGNS FOR THE GARDEN

Barbecue
A beautiful, sturdy structure complete with an arch and chimney

Storage seat
A dual-purpose feature—good for concealing garden bits and pieces

Raised herringbone patio
An easy patio to build, with great decorative value

Classic round pond
The perfect habitat for goldfish

Gateway columns
Used to create an imposing entrance

Simple garden wall
Can be used to define changing levels

Decorative raised bed
A good way of softening an otherwise formal patio

Tudor arch wall niche
An intriguing feature that is sure to become a talking point

Planted patio
Home for small plants such as roses or herbs

Classic birdbath
Built within view of the house, for winter interest

Semicircular steps
Cleverly draw attention to the front door

Waterspout
Fun to look at and a safe water feature for a household with children

Strawberry barrel
The perfect container for growing strawberries

Feature wall
An exciting, artistic feature wall incorporating different motifs

Country cottage path
A colorful, simple way to construct a traditional path

Flower border edging
As well as being attractive, the edging allows for easy mowing of the lawn

LEFT **This garden plan demonstrates how the projects in this book might be used to fill your garden with attractive brickwork designs.**

Tools

You don't need many tools for brickwork, but they should be the best tools that you can afford. If you are working to a fixed budget, purchase top-quality trowels (a mason's trowel and a pointing trowel) and a level (a traditional wood-cased one is best), and then save money by buying cheap shovels and suchlike. The following pages describe essential items for the toolbox, and tools you may want to rent to make a job easier.

FOR YOUR OWN PROTECTION

Gloves

Goggles

Dust-mask

Ear defenders

Protecting your hands and feet

Brickwork—digging holes, breaking up hardpan, and handling bricks—is tough on your hands, so wear hefty leather gloves whenever possible. You will probably have to take them off for fiddly jobs. When mixing concrete and mortar, wear waterproof, thick rubber gloves, which will protect your skin from contact with corrosive cement powder. Boots made from stout leather, ideally with reinforced metal toecaps, will protect your feet.

More protection

Sometimes it is necessary to wear additional protective gear, especially when you are cutting materials that generate sharp chips and a lot of dust. Wear goggles when smashing hardpan and cutting or breaking bricks, stone, and concrete, and a dust-mask when mixing cement powder. When using a circular saw with a masonry blade, wear heavy boots, gloves, goggles, a dust-mask, and ear defenders. Wear ear defenders when using any noisy machine.

TOOLS FOR MEASURING AND MARKING

Big tape measure

Small tape measure

Pegs and string

Level

Measuring and marking out a site

If you are unfamiliar with garden projects and brickwork, it can be difficult to know how to begin. Everything starts from a footing, so either build on an existing footing such as a patio (see page 21), or dig out some earth and make a new footing.

When building a footing, use a tape measure (available in various lengths) to establish the dimensions, then mark the site with pegs and string (see page 21). If the shape is irregular, use marking chalk or spray paint. Dig out the footing hole: the sides of the hole contain the footing. Alternatively, wooden boards (formwork) can be used to construct an accurate frame to retain the footing. A level is used when digging to a level depth. Spoil should be removed from the site.

Measuring and marking during construction

The exact dimensions of brickwork projects are (or should be) governed by the proportions of a brick (see page 17), so you can either calculate the length and width of the first course, and mark it out on the new or existing footing using a tape measure, long rule, and a piece of chalk; or arrange the bricks without mortar, judging the gaps between each brick, then nudge the layout straight and square and mark around it with chalk.

Once you have laid the first course of bricks, use a level to indicate the horizontal and vertical positions, and a long rule to check for straightness. A line set (a line stretched between two pegs) is useful for guiding the courses of stone, and estimating course heights, on long lengths of wall (see page 66).

TOOLS FOR MAKING FOOTINGS

Sledgehammer

Wheelbarrow

Bucket

Garden rake

Spade   *Fork*   *Shovel*

Removing sod and digging earth

Once the area of ground has been marked with string, chalk, or paint, start digging and removing earth to create a clean-sided hole of a specific depth. A spade is used to slice through the sod, and a fork is very handy for removing the sod in square chunks. A wheelbarrow is essential for moving earth away from the site, and a bucket is useful for removing small quantities and when working in confined areas. The wheelbarrow and bucket are also employed for moving all other materials. To dig a hole in extremely hard or stony ground, specialist digging tools such as a pick or mattock may be required.

Compacting hardpan

Hardpan (waste brick, stone, and concrete) must be compacted in order to form a firm base. A sledgehammer is used to break it up into smaller pieces and to beat these into the ground to make a compact, even layer. This can be notoriously hard work when dealing with large areas (over 20 sq. feet), so either get help or buy broken-brick hardpan, which is easier to break and consolidate. Always wear goggles to protect your eyes from chips.

Spreading gravel, sand, and concrete

Use a shovel for spreading gravel, sand, ballast (a mixture of gravel and sand), and concrete. A rake is useful for spreading dry materials evenly over a large area. A screed strip is brought in to scrape off excess material to make a smooth and level surface to a specific depth, and is used for concrete, sand, and ballast. It consists of a length of wood supported at either end by a frame (see page 40). Some patio footings consist of dry materials, laid down without cement, and it is best to hire a compacting machine called a power tamper to compress gravel, sand, or ballast into a firm base (also for firming patio bricks into position).

TOOLS FOR MIXING CONCRETE AND MORTAR

Mixing by hand

Mixing concrete or mortar by hand is hard work. Find a sheet of exterior plywood for mixing on, about 12 foot square and ½–1 inch thick, a shovel, and a bucket for the water (see pages 22–23). If more than 55 pounds of cement or mortar is required, you should seriously consider using a cement mixer.

Using a cement mixer

A cement mixer is used for making concrete and mortar, and is a wonderful timesaver that actually does a better job than you can do by hand. Cement mixers can be bought or rented, and are available in different capacities, powered by an electric or petrol engine. The small, electric versions are most suitable for do-it-yourself projects and mix up to about 12 shovelfuls of portland cement, sand, or ballast, producing one wheelbarrow load of concrete or mortar. Follow the directions supplied with the machine. Remember that at the end of a job, an empty cement mixer can be left for only about five minutes before it needs washing out, otherwise the remnants of cement will set solid. Use a hose and a brush to do this.

TOOLS FOR HANDLING MORTAR

Pointing trowel

Bricklayer's trowel

Spreading mortar

The mason's trowel (the larger of the two similarly shaped trowels) is the one used most frequently in bricklaying. It is used to scoop up mortar and spread it smoothly, to an even thickness, over the top and ends of the bricks, and also for slicing off excess mortar that has squeezed out from between the bricks. It can also be employed to knock the bricks level (using the blade or the handle) or to chop bricks roughly in half.

Finishing joints

After the bricks have been laid and before the mortar is dry, the joints between the bricks need to be tidied up with a pointing trowel or by another method (see page 27). The pointing trowel is used to fill any gaps in the joints, and also to repoint (see page 31). Be careful not to smear the excess mortar on the face of the brickwork. The pointing trowel may be used in place of the bricklayer's trowel if you find that too heavy and awkward.

TOOLS FOR CUTTING BRICK, STONE, AND CONCRETE

Circular saw with a masonry blade

Brick chisel

Stonemason's hammer

Brick hammer

Cutting bricks

To cut just a few bricks, for the projects in this book, we recommend using hand tools for the sake of simplicity. The most common method is to simply chop the bricks with a brick chisel and stonemason's hammer (see page 24).

Various machines are available for cutting brick and masonry (see page 25). You can use a circular saw fitted with an abrasive masonry blade, an angle grinder, brick guillotine (good for quick 90° cuts, but the results aren't as good as with a masonry saw), or a disk cutter fitted with a stone-cutting disk. If your design requires hundreds of bricks to be cut, consider hiring a masonry saw with a diamond blade (which will also cope with angled cuts).

CAUTION

Circular saws with masonry blades and other handheld disk cutters are dangerous machines and should be operated only while wearing protective gear (see page 25). Follow the manufacturer's advice, and if you have never operated one before, it's advisable to ask an expert or the tool rental store to show you how to use it safely.

Cutting blocks, slabs, stone, and tiles

Concrete block pavers can be cut in the same way as bricks, as described above. Concrete slab pavers, flat pieces of stone, and thick concrete or clay tiles can all be cut with a heavyweight disk cutter or masonry saw (depending on size). However, for safety reasons we recommend using a small circular saw fitted with a stone-cutting disk to score a cut, and then finishing the cut with a brick chisel and stonemason's hammer (see page 24). Most thin tiles can be cut with a basic hand-operated tile-cutting machine.

Wear gloves and goggles when cutting by hand; if using a machine, wear gloves, goggles, a dust-mask, ear defenders, and stout boots.

ADDITIONAL TOOLS

Handsaw

Jigsaw

Twist drill bit

Masonry drill bit

Power drill

Screwdriver

Wire brush

Paintbrush

Claw hammer

Rubber mallet

Gardening trowel

Scissors

Woodwork

Sometimes the projects require you to use formwork (wooden frames) during the casting of footings. Formwork usually consists of planks of wood laid square and level, held in place by pegs and nails (see page 19). A handsaw (or crosscut saw) and a claw hammer are all that is needed to make it.

Simple brickwork arches are easy to build as long as you use a wooden former to establish the shape of the arch and support the bricks during the building process (see pages 94–99, 108–113, 114–119, 120–125). The former is made from plywood cut with an electric jigsaw, which is a safe and easy-to-use tool. After drawing the curved shape on the plywood (you may use a trammel former for this—see page 27), hold down the plywood on the work-bench, start up the saw (don't let the blade touch the wood until the motor is running) and gently guide the blade around the curve. Wear goggles and follow the manufacturer's directions.

Drilling holes

A general-purpose power drill with hammer action is ideal for drilling jobs. For drilling wood, use twist bits for small-diameter holes (under $3/8$ inch in diameter), and flat or spade bits for larger holes. For drilling into brickwork and masonry, use masonry bits and set the drill to hammer mode. Always follow the directions supplied with the tool.

Finishing

Once you have completed a project (or at the end of each day if you are conscientious), you will need to clear up the site and clean any blobs, splashes, and smears of mortar off the brickwork and ground. Use a wire brush to scrub bricks (wear gloves and goggles). If you choose to apply a treatment to the surface of the brickwork in order to clean it (see page 31), use a paintbrush. A paintbrush is also used for any painting tasks such as sealing render with tank-sealer, as in the water feature on page 125.

Miscellaneous

A rubber mallet is useful for bedding brickwork or masonry in mortar. It is soft, but heavy, and does the job without damaging the surface of the material. The wooden or plastic-covered handle of a stonemason's hammer or brick hammer will do a similar job. Other useful tools include a screwdriver for driving in screws (if you prefer them to nails) and a gardener's trowel for projects such as the Decorative Raised Bed and the Strawberry Barrel, where planting is required.

When building water features that employ lining materials, such as the Classic Round Pond, use scissors to cut the lining materials; use a hacksaw (a metal saw) to cut the armored plastic cable used to protect electric cable and water pipes, in projects such as the Waterspout. Don't buy new tools until the need arises.

Materials

For garden projects, it is best to use exterior-grade bricks, or building bricks (rated **MW/MX** or **SW/SX**), both of which are harder than standard bricks, with good frost resistance. Your first search, therefore, will be for a supplier who can provide good-quality bricks at low cost. You can cut costs dramatically by hiring a flatbed and going to the supplier yourself. If you are lucky, there will be misshapes available at half the normal price—these bruised and battered bricks are perfect for garden projects. Avoid bricks that show cracks across their width.

BRICKS

Handmade rustic

Handmade facing

Extruded common

Extruded semibuilding

Header splay

Single bullnose

Angled coping

Half-round coping

"Terra-cotta" classical panel

Appearance

For most people, the most important aspect of brickwork is its appearance. Generally speaking, bricks are more attractive than other manufactured walling materials such as concrete or reconstituted stone. Use discretion when choosing bricks: some combinations of color and texture in modern bricks are ugly.

Study examples of finished brickwork to identify the types you like most. Remember the characteristics of a brick are intensified when many bricks are placed together in a wall or patio. Bricks vary from area to area, because they are made from clay dug from the ground, and this varies in color and properties. They are also manufactured in different ways: machine-made bricks are the most accurately formed and easy to build with; handmade bricks look better but are a bit wobbly and more difficult to lay. The design and availability of special bricks varies according to region.

Properties

Bricks are manufactured for different purposes. "Facing" bricks are sold for their appearance. "Building" bricks are intended for situations where high strength and low water absorption are very important, and are not sold for their appearance. This type of brick is the most expensive, and you would probably choose it only for a particular situation, such as when building steps, because its extra strength and hardness guarantee that the edges of the steps will not crumble.

All bricks have a frost-resistance rating, varying from frost resistant (SW or SX), to moderately frost resistant (MW or MX), and nonfrost resistant (NW, only to be used internally). We have used moderately frost-resistant facing bricks for the projects.

Bricks have six sides: two end or "header" faces, two side or "stretcher" faces, a top or "frog" face, and a bottom face. Most bricks have some kind of cavity to trap mortar—the frog is a rectangular recess in the top for this purpose (some bricks have three holes running right through the brick instead). Bricks with frogs are more versatile, as they have one flat surface that lets them be used upside down as coping or paving.

Sizes

The dimensions of a brick are significant, and when you start building, you will realize why. They are a convenient size to handle, roughly twice as long as they are wide, and their height is roughly one third of their length. This means that they fit together perfectly in many different ways. Imperial and metric bricks may vary, and some bricks are made to match the size of old bricks.

Imperial bricks are normally 8 in long, 3¾ in wide, and 2¼ in thick. When calculating the number of bricks required for brickwork, ¼ in mortar joints are allowed for, giving a unit measurement of 8¼ in long, 4 in wide, and 2½ in thick.

Metric bricks are normally 215 mm long, 102.5 mm wide, and 65 mm thick. Allowing for 10 mm mortar joints, this gives a unit measurement of 225 mm long, 112.5 mm, wide and 75 mm thick.

All the projects can be built using either imperial or metric bricks. As with any DIY project, always calculate and measure quantities carefully, and be prepared to make adjustments to your projects to accommodate variations in brick sizes.

Other kinds of brick

If you want to use old bricks from a salvage yard, because you like their antique appearance, or want to match existing brickwork, be prepared to pay more than for new bricks. Avoid bricks with mortar still stuck to them, because it is tough work to chisel off.

"Seconds" (second quality) are bricks that are less than perfect—usually chipped, warped, cracked, or damaged by under- or overfiring. Avoid cracked or underfired bricks.

Many special brick shapes are available for specific and decorative purposes—see what's on offer and consider incorporating these into your projects to give added interest.

BUYING TIPS

- Never buy bricks without inspecting the product.
- When buying seconds, ideally it is best to select each brick individually.
- If you are hiring a flatbed to collect the bricks yourself, it is much better to make several journeys with small loads, rather than a single journey with an overloaded vehicle.
- If you are having bricks delivered, plan in advance where they are to be unloaded, and make sure that they are not going to pose a hazard or obstruction.

FOOTING MATERIALS, MORTAR, AND RENDER

   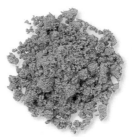 

Ballast *Gravel* *Sharp sand* *Soft sand* *Portland cement*

Concrete, aggregates, and ballast

Most footings begin with hardpan—waste brick, stone, and concrete, which is broken into pieces and compacted to provide a firm, interlocked base that promotes water drainage. Normally, the footing is completed with a layer of concrete.

Concrete consists of portland cement powder, fine aggregate (sand), coarse aggregate (gravel or crushed stone), and water. The shape and size of the particles of sand and stone in the aggregate decide the character of the concrete—its strength, hardness, durability, and porosity. Ready-mixed aggregate can be bought in most suppliers. This mix of aggregates (sharp sand and small stones or gravel) is often called ballast. For the projects, pick an average mix made up from small-sized gravel and sand.

Some footings for patios and paths omit the concrete—alternative footings are: hardpan, gravel, and sand; hardpan and ballast; or hardpan, ballast, and sand. In each case, the hardpan, ballast, and sand are compacted.

Sand

Sand is available in various types. Sharp ("building") sand is coarse and is often used for making concrete, laying under paving, or is mixed with portland cement to make mortar for rendering (see below). Soft ("mason's") sand is a medium sand used for making mortar. It can also be used for concrete and footings (it is not as effective as sharp sand, but you may want to order one type of sand in bulk to do the whole job). Fine ("silver") sand is ideal for filling the joints in brick and block paving (but use ordinary sand for large gaps).

Mortar

Mortar is a mixture of soft sand, cement powder, and water, and is used to stick bricks together. The ratio of ingredients is important and mixing needs practice (see pages 22–23). A mortar made with sharp sand produces a coarser mortar suitable for rendering. Render is a thin coating of mortar stuck to the surface of bricks.

TILES, STONE, AND PAVERS

Roof tile

Floor tile

Decorative glazed tile

Clay block paver

Concrete paving slab

Reconstituted stone paving slab

Millstone

Real stone slab

York stone

Roof stone

Real stone block

Cobblestones

Boulder

Pebbles

Tiles

A huge range of tiles is available. Clay roof tiles are traditionally used as a coping to finish the top of brickwork structures and help deflect rainwater away from the structure. Decorative clay tiles, designed specifically for brickwork, can be obtained from specialty suppliers. (Those that display a floral decoration are sometimes known as rose blocks.) Some concrete tiles are described as reconstituted stone, because they are made to look like real clay or stone. Terra-cotta floor tiles, quarry tiles, brightly colored tiles, or patterned glazed tiles can all be incorporated into brickwork to make a decorative design.

Stone

Stone is traditionally combined with brick for decorative effect. Many kinds of real stone are available, but it is often best to choose a type that is quarried in your area, because it will harmonize with the color of local bricks. See what your supplier has in stock and look at local examples of building to help you choose. Avoid stone that looks crumbly or cracked. Try to select pieces that can be used as they stand, in order to avoid having to cut them. (If cutting is necessary, see pages 24–25.)

Cobblestones and pebbles may be bedded in mortar to create a patterned surface that complements brickwork or paving.

Paving slabs

Straightforward concrete paving slabs may be too plain for garden projects, but there are many attractive alternatives. Textured and colored slabs, or reconstituted stone slabs (a mixture of crushed stone and concrete) can look as good as real stone. Real stone paving slabs are wonderful, but extremely expensive, so your budget may not be able to accommodate them.

Pavers

You can use standard bricks for paving (to match nearby brick-work), but the cavities (frogs or holes) will need filling with sand and the bricks cannot be laid with equal gaps between them, because their proportions are designed to incorporate mortar joints—however, this sometimes adds to their charm.

Pavers (or paviors) are extremely hard, thin clay or concrete bricks designed specifically for paths, patios, and drives. They come in many shapes, sizes, and finishes. Perhaps the most attractive and durable option is the kiln-fired, brick-sized clay paver, in subtle colors that never fade. (Concrete pavers fade in color after five to ten years.) Pavers are exactly twice as long as they are wide, and are usually thinner than a brick, which makes them easier to lay in patterns. The recess required to lay them is shallower than that needed for bricks. Concrete pavers include imitation stone setts (small rectangular paving blocks), and mock bricks.

LUMBER AND PLYWOOD

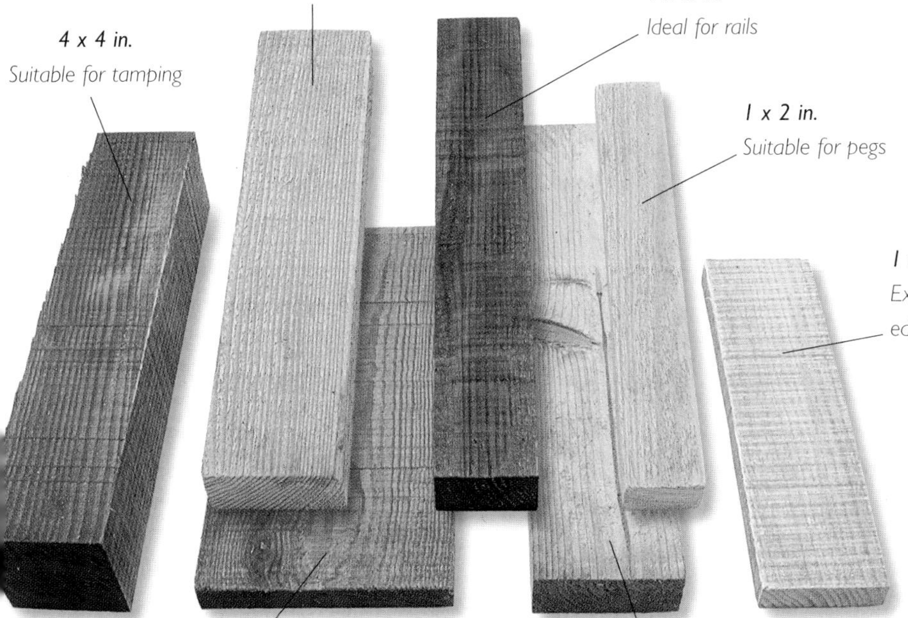

1 x 3 in.
Good for framing

1 x 2 in.
Ideal for rails

4 x 4 in.
Suitable for tamping

1 x 2 in.
Suitable for pegs

1 x 3 in.
Excellent for edging paths

Plywood

1 x 6 in.
Suitable for formwork

Useful lumber sections

2 x 4 in.
Good for edging small slabs

Railroad tie

Formwork

Formwork is the wooden framing used to make a footing. Use cheap, ready-sawn or reclaimed lumber, as it will be ruined by the cement and usually serves no purpose after the footing is complete. Plywood consists of thin layers of wood stuck together, and is ideal for making formers, which are the arched frames used to support brickwork arches during construction. It comes in standard-size sheets of 8 x 4 ft., or smaller pieces cut from it.

Other uses

Wood goes well with brick—the warm colors look good together. Treated pine, oak, or railroad fties can be incorporated into your garden projects.

During the construction process, cheap exterior-grade plywood (often called "shuttering" plywood) can be used to protect the area surrounding a project, guarding lawns and drives against general mess and damage.

MISCELLANEOUS

Some projects, especially the Classic Round Pond and the Water-spout, use more materials than shown here. Specialty materials such as synthetic padding and butyl rubber may not be available at your home improvement center. Look up suppliers in a directory of local businesses (synthetic padding and butyl rubber are sold by suppliers of pond-building materials and water features).

Footings

When it comes to building footings, you can't cut costs. Most projects need a solid, no-nonsense concrete footing. If you suspect that the conditions in your garden mean that a stronger than average footing is required, adjustments to the basic footing can be made. For example, if the ground is soft, simply make the footing wider and deeper, or if the ground is very wet, lay extra hardpan to increase drainage.

ABOUT FOOTINGS

Every brickwork project requires a footing of some kind. A footing is a strong, stable, level base on which to build. It would be no good laying bricks directly on the ground, because their weight, together with rainwater, would compress and erode the soil, causing the brick structure to sink, crack, lean over, and fall apart.

So whether you are constructing a wall, a birdbath, or a patio, start by building a good footing. Footings are usually made from hardpan topped by concrete. Footings for patios and paths often omit the concrete and substitute other materials. Sometimes it is possible to use an existing footing (see box).

TYPES OF FOOTING

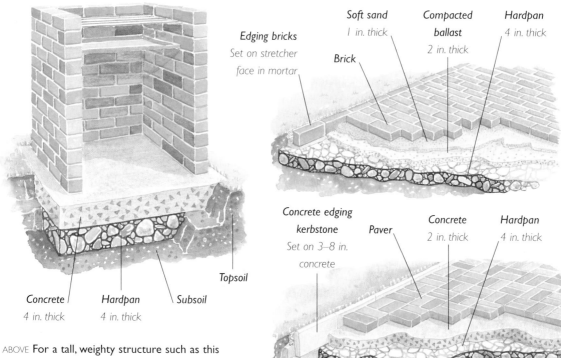

Edging bricks
Set on stretcher
face in mortar

Soft sand
1 in. thick

Brick

Compacted ballast
2 in. thick

Hardpan
4 in. thick

LEFT **A footing for a brick patio on firm, well-drained ground. On a patio with a large area, a power tamper is used to compress the layers.**

Concrete edging kerbstone
Set on 3–8 in. concrete

Paver

Concrete
2 in. thick

Hardpan
4 in. thick

LEFT **A footing for a paver patio on moist, soft ground. The thickness of the hardpan should be increased to 8 in. if water is moving across the site.**

Topsoil

Concrete
4 in. thick

Hardpan
4 in. thick

Subsoil

ABOVE **For a tall, weighty structure such as this barbecue, a generous slab of concrete has been set on compacted hardpan.**

Most brickwork walls, and upright structures such as barbecues and planters, need a strong hardpan and concrete footing as illustrated above left.

For paving projects—patios and paths—the footing can consist of hardpan and a dryish mix of concrete or, alternatively, hardpan and compacted layers of other materials (although not as solid as concrete, this footing is adequate for domestic patios and paths, and less work to make). This alternative footing can be made of hardpan, gravel, and sand; hardpan and ballast; or hardpan, ballast, and sand. In each case, the hardpan, ballast, and sand are compacted. However, if the ground is soft, sandy, or boggy, it is better to include concrete in the footing. Also, if the design of the project means that it will be awkward to use the power tamper required for compacting the materials, opt for a concrete footing. Edging bricks or blocks need to be stuck down with mortar or contained by a kerb.

MEASURING, MARKING, AND DIGGING

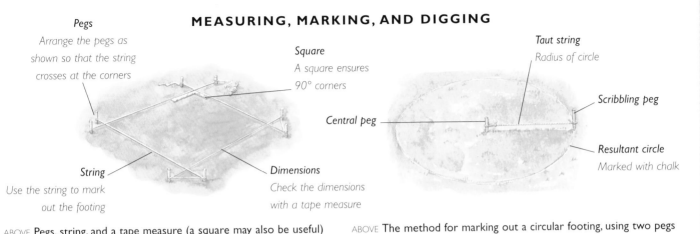

Pegs
Arrange the pegs as
shown so that the string
crosses at the corners

Square
A square ensures
90° corners

Central peg

String
Use the string to mark
out the footing

Dimensions
Check the dimensions
with a tape measure

Taut string
Radius of circle

Scribbling peg

Resultant circle
Marked with chalk

ABOVE Pegs, string, and a tape measure (a square may also be useful) are used to mark out a rectangular area of the correct size.

ABOVE The method for marking out a circular footing, using two pegs and a length of string, plus some chalk.

Work out the exact size of the footing (for example, although a patio footing is the same size as the finished patio, a wall footing needs to be wider than a wall) and its precise depth. To establish the depth, survey the site (if the ground slopes, knock a peg in the ground to indicate the chosen finished level of the footing) and draw a cross-section of the construction (visualize the project sliced across the middle with a knife) to help calculate the depth of soil that should be removed.

Mark out rectangular areas using pegs, string, and a tape measure. If the footing is an L-shape or other complex shape, divide it into a series of rectangles. To check the accuracy of a

rectangle, first make sure the opposite sides are of equal length. Measure the diagonals, then add them together and divide by two. This tells you how long a diagonal should be in a shape with 90° corners. To make the diagonals equal, adjust the pegs' positions.

For circular footings, bang a peg into the ground at the center. Make a length of string with a loop at each end (the length from loop to loop should be the same as the radius of the circle). Slip one loop over the central peg, then insert another peg into the other end and use it to scribe out a circle. Mark the circle using spray paint, chalk powder, or chalk. Dig out the footing as described on page 13.

LAYING FOOTINGS

The initial layer of most footings consists of hardpan, which is broken and compacted with a sledgehammer to make a firm base. The second layer of a footing for upright structures, such as a wall or barbecue, is usually concrete. Wooden formwork is normally laid to contain it. Pegs are nailed to the outer side of boards and knocked through the hardpan into the ground, so that they are level with each other. The boards indicate where the top of the

concrete should be. When the concrete is laid, a length of wood is used to scrape away excess concrete and tamp it level. For many paving projects, the second layer might consist of gravel, followed by a layer of sand compacted to just below the finished level of the footing. This is topped with loose sand. (For footings larger then 10 ft. in either direction, divide up the area with extra boards set to the finished height of the footing.)

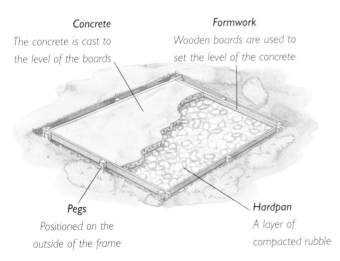

Concrete
The concrete is cast to
the level of the boards

Formwork
Wooden boards are used to
set the level of the concrete

Pegs
Positioned on the
outside of the frame

Hardpan
A layer of
compacted rubble

ABOVE This footing is designed to be set flush with the ground. A formwork frame is used to contain the concrete.

USING EXISTING FOOTINGS

If a brickwork feature is small, it is sometimes possible to build it on an existing area of paving. Before you do that, if possible check what is underneath the paving by lifting a few bricks, blocks, or slabs. If the footing looks poor, lift the paving in the area you need to build on, then dig out extra soil and make a proper footing, replacing the original paving afterward. Once you are satisfied that the area is solid, check that it is level. Small discrepancies can be compensated for by adding extra mortar under the first course of bricks. If the slope is too great (more than 3/8 in. across the length of the brickwork), cast a level concrete slab on top, no less than 1 1/2 in. thick, on which to build.

Concrete and mortar

Concrete and mortar are two very important components in brickwork construction. Concrete is used in footings and mortar is used to stick bricks together, and for rendering. They are both made from mixing dry ingredients, including portland cement powder, with water. For successful mixtures, it is important to get the right ratio of ingredients and correct amount of water. For the most part, you can use a shovel to measure out dry ingredients.

ABOUT CONCRETE AND MORTAR

At first, you may look at a concrete or mortar mix and wonder how it is going to work, but it will set solid overnight and gain strength slowly over a few days. Mortar needs to be soft and buttery, so that it slices and cuts, and stays where it has been put without oozing or dribbling. However, the exact consistency required will depend on the absorbency of the bricks, and the humidity of the weather on the day. As with cooking the perfect loaf, follow the recipe to the letter, but be ready to make adjustments to suit changing needs. If the weather is dry, spray the bricks and mortar with a fine mist of water as you work.

MIXING METHODS FOR CONCRETE AND MORTAR

<table>
<tr><td>

CAUTION

Portland cement and lime are corrosive and can seriously burn the skin. Always wear goggles and gloves, and wash your hands and face after working with them.
</td></tr>
</table>

For quantities that use more than 55 lb. of portland cement powder, we recommend that you rent a cement mixer.

Mixing in a wheelbarrow

1 Use a shovel to measure out the dry ingredients into the wheelbarrow—first the sand or ballast, and then the portland cement. Continue until you have enough or the barrow is half-full. Turn the ingredients over several times until they are thoroughly mixed.

2 Pour about one-third of a bucket of water into one end of the wheelbarrow, then drag small amounts of the dry ingredients into the water. Repeat the process until all the water has been soaked up by the dry ingredients.

3 Turn over the whole heap several times, all the while adding small amounts of water, until you can chop it into clean, wet slices.

Mixing on a board

1 Measure the dry ingredients onto a board with a shovel—first the sand or ballast, then the cement. Mix until it is an even color.

2 Dig a hole in the center and pour in about half a bucket of water. Work round the heap, dragging small amounts of the dry materials into the water. If the water threatens to break over the rim, swiftly pull in more of the dry materials to stem the flow.

3 When the water has been soaked up, add more until the concrete or mortar is the correct consistency. The finished mixture should form crisp, firm slices that stand up under their own weight without crumbling.

Mixing
Drag the dry materials into the water

ABOVE It is often convenient to use a wheelbarrow for mixing mortar; remember to give it a good clean afterward.

Mixing
Make a hole in the heap and add a small amount of water

ABOVE When mixing on a board, drag the dry materials into the water in the center of the heap. Try not to let the water escape.

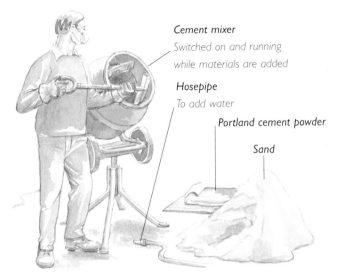

ABOVE Use a shovel to measure quantities: for example, one shovelful (1 part) of cement powder to four shovelfuls (4 parts) of sand.

Mixing using a cement mixer

Follow the instructions supplied with the machine and use an electricity circuit breaker safety device between the plug and socket. Measure out the sand or ballast using a shovel, then switch on the mixer and put it straight into the machine. Don't overfill: a small machine can take about 10–12 shovelfuls (including cement powder). Add the portland cement. After a few minutes, when the ingredients are evenly mixed, start adding water a little at a time, until the correct consistency is achieved. (See box on recipes.)

GENERAL HANDLING OF CONCRETE AND MORTAR

It is best to use buckets to move a small quantity of concrete or mortar, and a wheelbarrow for large amounts. Make sure that the load is balanced. Two half-buckets are easier to move than one bucket that is full to overflowing. The same goes for a wheelbarrow: it's easier to move two small loads than it is to move a barrow that is so full that it slops and spills when you jolt over a bump. In most instances, a shovel is the best tool for unloading your cargo, although a small spade is good for filling up buckets.

WEATHER CONDITIONS

Concrete and mortar like to cure slowly—the longer, the better. If the weather is anything other than cool and damp, then to a lesser or greater extent you need to protect both concrete and mortar. If you have just built a wall and it's so hot that you can see the mortar drying out, cover it with damp newsprint. If the sun is blazing down on newly laid concrete, cover it with wet sacking and spray it at regular intervals over the next day or so. If you are expecting a night frost, cover both concrete and mortar with dry sacking, layers of newsprint, or sheets of plastic. If it starts to rain heavily, cover everything with sheets of plastic.

CONCRETE AND MORTAR RECIPES

Ingredients are measured by volume (in the projects, weights are given only as a guide to ordering materials, since volumes of different materials vary in weight, and sand and ballast are heavier when wet). "Parts" signify the ratios of ingredients (by volume) to each other, measured in the same manner (such as by the shovelful). So a recipe listing 1 part portland cement and 4 parts sand, means 1 shovelful of portland cement and 4 shovelfuls of sand, or 2 shovelfuls of portland cement and 8 shovelfuls of sand, depending on the quantity you are mixing. Recipes do vary, but we recommend the following proportions.

Concrete for footings

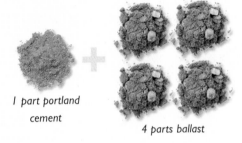

1 part portland cement

4 parts ballast

Mix 1 part portland cement with 4 parts ballast. Add water and mix to the consistency of stiff mashed potatoes. You can substitute 2 parts sharp sand and 3 parts aggregate for 4 parts ballast. (You may wish to do this if you bought these materials in bulk and want to use them instead of ordering ballast.)

Dryish mix of concrete for paving footings

As above, except that a lot less water is added—just enough to damp down the dry ingredients. The mixture will absorb moisture from the air and set after a few days.

Mortar for bricklaying and pointing

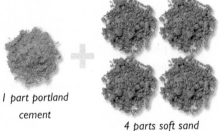

1 part portland cement

4 parts soft sand

Mix 1 part portland cement with 4 parts soft sand. Add water and mix to the consistency of mashed potatoes. For exposed sites where strong winds and heavy rain may erode the mortar, 1 part portland cement and 3 parts sand is commonly used.

Dryish mix of mortar for paving joints

As above, except a lot less water is added (add water as described for dryish mix of concrete).

Cutting brick, stone, and concrete

In many ways, the sign of a good brickworker is the ability to place bricks for best fit without having to cut many

of them. When you do need to make a cut, it must be accurate. For the most part, you will be using a stonemason's

hammer and brick chisel to cut bricks into halves and fourths. To cut concrete slabs and tiles, it might be necessary

to use an electric circular saw with a masonry blade. Clay tiles can be cut with a heavy-duty ceramic tile cutter.

CUTTING BRICKS

HOW TO AVOID TOO MUCH CUTTING

- Plan the length and width of the structure—path or wall—so that it is made up from a number of whole bricks.
- If you are using a mixture of materials—such as bricks and tiles, or bricks and concrete slabs—make sure that the module sizes of each are compatible.
- Avoid using a mixture of imperial and metric bricks, unless there is a good reason to do so.
- Choose a bond that works without the need to cut bricks.
- Go for structures that are rectilinear in plan view, rather than triangular or hexagonal, for example.
- If you want to use a bond that requires bricks to be cut, at least choose one that only requires you to cut bricks in half.

Mason's trowel
Also known as a
builder's trowel

Brick
Must be
held securely

Line of cut

ABOVE Give the brick a firm, well-placed blow with the edge of the mason's trowel and it should fall in two.

Cutting bricks with a mason's trowel or brick hammer

The most basic way of cutting a brick is with a mason's trowel: hold the brick in one hand and strike it firmly with the edge of the trowel. If you are lucky, the brick will fall in half. If it doesn't, repeat the procedure on the other face.

To use a brick hammer, simply hold the brick in one hand—so that the waste end is pointing away from your body—and then use the chisel end of the brick hammer to clip away at the waste until you have cut back to the mark. Work little by little, backing up to the line of cut.

Brick hammer

Chisel end
of hammer
Used to nibble
away at the waste

Work little
by little

ABOVE Work with a pecking action, gradually nibbling back the brick to the marked line of cut.

Cutting bricks with a brick chisel

A more accurate way of cutting bricks is by using a stonemason's hammer and brick chisel. This is the method used most frequently in small brickwork projects. Position the brick on something soft, such as a pad of old carpet, or on the lawn, to help absorb the shock of the blow. Wear goggles and strong leather gloves. Take the brick chisel in one hand and the stonemason's hammer in the other, and set the edge of the chisel firmly on the line of cut, so that it is upright and square with the brick. Finally, give the chisel a single, well-placed blow with the hammer and the brick should fall in half. It may be wise to practice on some old bricks first.

Glove
Thick leather
glove worn for
protection

Stonemason's hammer

Brick chisel
Has a rubber
guard around
the head

RIGHT Set the brick chisel on the line of cut and give it a single, well-placed blow with the stonemason's hammer.

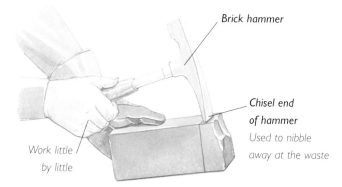
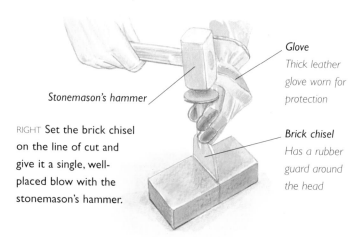

Cutting bricks with a machine

There are various machines you can use to cut bricks:

- Circular saw with a masonry blade (handheld power tool).
- Angle grinder fitted with a stone-cutting disk. Use in the same way as a circular saw.
- Brick guillotine. To use a guillotine cutter, mark the brick where you want to cut it and place it on the platform below the chisel-like blade. Pull down on the lever.
- Disk cutter fitted with a stone-cutting disk (a disk cutter normally describes a large angle grinder). To use, follow the directions for a circular saw with masonry blade (see below).
- Masonry saw. To use a masonry saw, place the machine on a level surface and set the brick on the platform, so that the line of cut is aligned with the marking guide, and then pull down on the lever so that the disk makes the cut.
- Machines are potentially dangerous—follow the manufacturer's directions carefully and always wear goggles, a dust-mask, and gloves. Ear defenders and stout boots are also recommended.

CUTTING TILES, STONE, AND CONCRETE

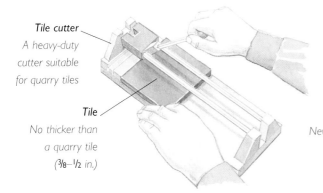

Tile cutter
A heavy-duty cutter suitable for quarry tiles

Tile
No thicker than a quarry tile (³⁄₈–¹⁄₂ in.)

ABOVE Having scored the line of cut, draw the handle back so that the anvil is centered on the tile, and press down on the lever.

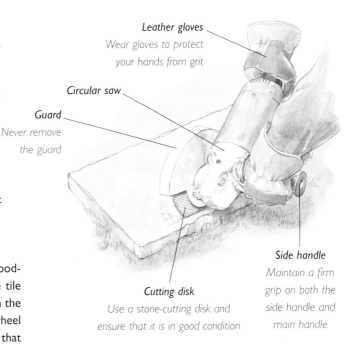

Leather gloves
Wear gloves to protect your hands from grit

Circular saw

Guard
Never remove the guard

Side handle
Maintain a firm grip on both the side handle and main handle

Cutting disk
Use a stone-cutting disk and ensure that it is in good condition

ABOVE Hold the circular saw firmly, and keeping your body well away from the line of cut, make repeated light passes to cut a groove.

Tiles

Clay tiles—roof tiles and quarry tiles—are best cut with a good-quality, heavy-duty ceramic tile cutter. All you do is butt the tile hard up against the stop, so that the line of cut is aligned with the handle, and then push the lever forward so that the little wheel scores the surface of the tile. Then you pull the lever back so that the anvil is bridged over the tile, and push down hard so that the tile snaps in half. Clear the debris after every cut.

Cutting stone and concrete with a circular saw

Set the slab flat on the lawn and use a tape measure and chalk to draw out the line of cut. Put on goggles, a dust-mask, ear defenders, and gloves. Hold the circular saw so that the wheel is at right angles to the slab. Brace yourself, then switch on the power and gently run the spinning disk forward, to lightly score along the marked cut. Make several runs to deepen the line of cut, then switch off the power and flip the slab over. Switch the power back on and re-run the whole procedure on the other side. Continue repeating the process until the slab of stone or concrete falls in two. During the whole cutting operation, always make sure that both you and the power cable remain well clear of the cutting disk. Always use a circuit breaker.

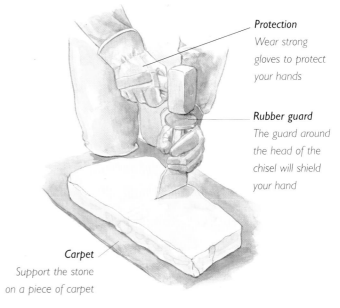

Protection
Wear strong gloves to protect your hands

Rubber guard
The guard around the head of the chisel will shield your hand

Carpet
Support the stone on a piece of carpet

ABOVE Cutting stone using a brick chisel and stonemason's hammer. Hold the chisel firmly on the mark and deliver a well-aimed blow.

Bricklaying

There can be something truly calming and therapeutic about bricklaying. The trick is to make sure that everything is well prepared, with the piles of bricks comfortably to hand, and the mortar at the ready, so that your rhythm of work is not broken. It is perfectly possible to cope with the work on your own, but if you can find a willing helper to pile up the bricks and mix the mortar, so much the better.

PLANNING THE COURSES

Walls and box structures

To build a wall, leave ³/₈ in. between each brick for mortar, and lay out a line of bricks to fit your chosen measurement in the best way. (If you are building a box structure, measure out the next side and repeat the procedure already described.) Lay the second course on the first so that the vertical joints are staggered. Working in this way, you will be able to plan out the structure without the need to cut bricks.

Circles, curves, and arches

Let's say that you want to build a circle or curve of bricks with a 40 in. radius. Take two

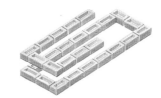

ABOVE Plan out the initial two courses of a box structure first.

ABOVE Half-bricks with tiles (left) and bricks set on edge (right).

wooden pegs and link them with string, so that they are 40 in. apart. Bang one peg in the ground, and use the other peg to indicate the circle. Lay the bricks (dry) around the circumference of the circle. When you come to the last brick, make adjustments to the gaps between each brick in the whole circle, to achieve a good fit. (The fit of the bricks can be planned on a scaled drawing, if you wish.) You may like to consider using half-bricks, or bricks laid on their stretcher (side) face, to create curved structures. If you are building an arch, plan it out on the ground before you start work, in order to avoid mistakes.

BASIC PROCEDURES

Setting out the line

Determine the line of the wall by banging in a peg at each end of the concrete footing. Take a length of string and run it over a piece of chalk, or through a container of chalk powder. Stretch the line between the pegs, about ¹/₈ in. above the ground, tying it so that it is taut and flush with the ground. When you are happy that the line is marking the course of the wall, lift it between finger and thumb and let it go with a snap, so that it slaps down a line of chalk on the concrete. (Alternatively, use a simple device called a chalk line, containing replaceable chalk, which deposits chalk on a string as you pull it out of the container.)

Applying mortar

Spread a line of mortar about ¹/₂ in. thick and 1 ¹/₈ in. long, and draw the point of the trowel through it to make a valley. Set the first brick in place and tap it with the handle of the trowel so that the excess squeezes out, and the mortar joint is about ³/₈ in. thick. Use the point of the trowel to push the excess mortar up onto the end of the brick to form the vertical joint, and then lay the second brick. Continue in this way until the end of the row. Check each course for height, and use the level vertically, horizontally, and diagonally to check that all the bricks are in line.

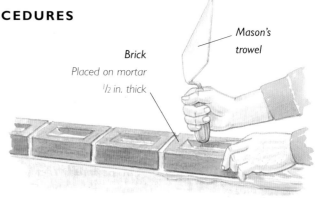

Mason's trowel

Brick
Placed on mortar
¹/₂ in. thick

ABOVE Set the brick carefully in place on the mortar and tap it level with the handle of the mason's trowel.

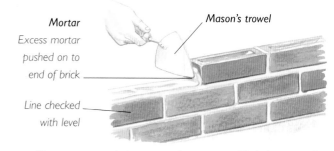

Mortar
Excess mortar pushed on to end of brick

Mason's trowel

Line checked with level

ABOVE There are several ways to apply mortar—this is just one of them. It is a good method for beginners.

THINGS TO AVOID

- On a hot day, don't use bricks dry: always dampen them so that they feel slightly less absorbent to the touch.
- Don't immediately scrape off excess mortar as it oozes out from between the bricks, because you will mark the bricks. It is much better to leave it until the bricks have absorbed the water from the mortar, and then scrape it off with the trowel.
- Don't use sharp sand, dirty sand, or stale portland cement to make mortar; use soft sand and fresh portland cement.
- Don't let the mortar on the trowels and level dry out—wash them every half hour or so.

ADDITIONAL TECHNIQUES

If you are finding it difficult to keep a uniform thickness of mortar between the joints when building a wall, a gauge rod will help. In effect, this is a cleat marked off along its length with alternate thicknesses for bricks and joints—2¼ in. for the height or thickness of the brick, ¼ in. for the thickness of the mortar, then 2¼ in., ¼ in., 2¼ in., and so on along the cleat. Simply stand this against the wall being built and use it to assess your progress, then make necessary adjustments by knocking the bricks harder or by adding more mortar.

Never assume that you can make mistakes here and there and make good at the end—you can't. It is important to be consistent and make sure that every brick is placed well.

USING A TRAMMEL FORMER

A trammel former is used when building circles or circle-based curves. It usually consists of a length of wood (trammel arm) drilled at one end, a block of wood the thickness of a brick (trammel support block), and a sheet of plywood (base). The support block is positioned on the base, surrounded by bricks to keep it in place. The trammel arm pivots on a

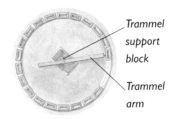

Trammel support block

Trammel arm

ABOVE If desired, a nail can be fixed to the arm as a pointer.

nail hammered into the support block. Each brick is placed so that it is aligned with the center of the circle and just touching the end of the arm. A U-shaped piece may be fixed to the arm to indicate the position of the edge bricks, which are laid to meet the end of the trammel former at 90°. There are also slightly different versions of the trammel former.

POINTING

ABOVE The joints between bricks need to be filled neatly with mortar. Use the edge of the trowel to wipe the mortar into the joint. Approach from both sides in order to create a peaked effect (mason's joint).

"Pointing" describes the finishing of the mortar joint between the bricks. There are four common finishes: raked or keyed, mason's, flat or flush, and weathered or struck. Pointing is done as the bricks are laid (avoid if the mortar is wet and sloppy), or when the wall is complete.

Raked joints are created by using a round bar, trowel handle, or another tool to run along the joint in order to hollow it. When using old bricks to build walls in the garden, the best finish is a raked joint: wait until the end of the day, and then use the point of the pointing trowel to swiftly rake the joint clear of excess mortar. This finish is perfect for a rustic cottage garden wall.

A mason's joint is formed by wiping the mortar into a peak. Flat joints are made by using the edge of the trowel to scrape the mortar off level with the bricks. In a weathered joint, the mortar is scraped out at an angle.

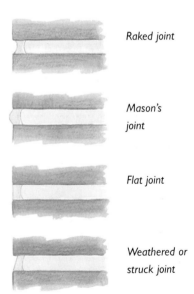

Raked joint

Mason's joint

Flat joint

Weathered or struck joint

INCORPORATING OTHER MATERIALS

In times past, brick walls were traditionally less uniform affairs, with bricks of varying thickness and much thicker joints. In some areas, it was common to stud wide joints with little pieces of stone or broken tiles. Rather than going to the trouble of cutting or rubbing bricks to create shaped bricks for arches, it was quite usual to use a stack of roof tiles or old quarry tiles to fill the space. In some coastal areas, it was common to stud joints with shells. Some builders incorporated specially shaped bricks.

Brick bonds and patterns

The pattern created by placing bricks to form a continuous wall, or laying them to form a patio surface, is known as the bond. The secret of creating a sound brick wall lies in the vertical joints of neighboring courses—these must be staggered. If vertical joints are not staggered, the structural integrity of the brickwork is at risk. There are various traditional bonds that achieve this. Look around your area for examples of brick patterns.

BASIC BONDS FOR WALLS AND STRUCTURES

Stretcher bond

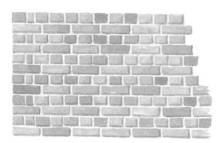

English bond

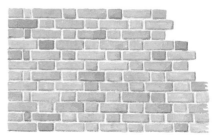

Flemish bond

The three primary bonds are stretcher bond, English bond, and Flemish bond. In a stretcher bond, each course is formed entirely of stretchers (side face of the brick), and it is suitable only for walls 3¾ in. (half a brick) thick. Each brick half-laps half its length on the bricks in the course below. A stretcher bond is great when you want to build a low structure or a cavity wall.

In an English bond, alternate courses show headers (end face of the brick) and stretchers. The end or head of the brick is centerd on the middle of the stretcher in the course below.

Flemish bond consists of alternate headers and stretchers in each course, with headers always being placed over the center of the stretcher below. Less common bonds are shown on the right.

SPECIAL BONDS

English garden wall bond

Heading bond

Flemish garden wall bond

Honeycomb bond

PATTERNS

Patterns on walls
Different colored bricks can be used to create a pattern, as in the English diaper tradition (an allover surface decoration of a small repeated pattern such as diamonds or squares, using colored, projecting, or recessed bricks). The way bricks are arranged can also create a pattern—either a self-pattern, as with a herringbone panel, or together with tiles.

Patterns on patios and paths
Patterns for patios and paths are created in much the same way as for walls, by brick color or arrangement. Because there are not the same concerns about structural integrity as for a wall, you can introduce additional elements, such as stones and shells, to create pattern, or use different thicknesses of brick.

Diaper pattern (darker color)

Diaper pattern (lighter color)

Herringbone band course

Raking tile courses

Walls and other structures

Brick walls are all around us—but next time you are out walking, notice how arches, columns, piers, and pillars can be used to lift a structure out of the ordinary, with a unique coming together of beauty and function. At its most basic, a brick wall can be one brick thick, just two or three courses high, and built on an existing footing. For a wall like this, the first course of bricks would just be bedded on mortar and the bricks cut to fit.

CONSTRUCTING WALLS

Supporting piers and buttresses
If you are building a freestanding wall from scratch, over three courses high, it needs a footing of compacted hardpan and a concrete slab, and piers about every 6 feet. If it is two bricks thick, the piers are adequate, but if you want to cut costs and build a single-brick-thick wall, supporting buttresses will also be needed about every 3 feet.

Corners and junctions
Corners and junctions are created by changing the direction of the bricks, arranging them in such a way that the corner or junction can be achieved without changing the bond. Right angles are the easiest to achieve.

Sloping sites
If the slope is gentle, dig a deep trench and lay a concrete slab below ground level, then build the

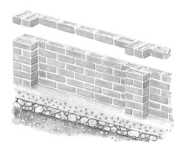

ABOVE A single-brick wall, with piers at regular intervals.

ABOVE A wall that runs up a slope needs a stepped footing.

wall. But if the slope is extreme, dig the trench and construct a stepped concrete slab (all below ground), making the concrete risers the same thickness as a brick (see lower illustration).

Curved walls
If the curve is big enough, the bricks can be nudged slightly so that the vertical joints open up and let the bricks run around the curve. But if the curve is tight, the easiest option is to either use half-bricks—like building an arch—or to stand the bricks on edge and build the wall from soldier courses.

Coping
A coping functions like a hat—it throws rain away from the face of the wall and stops it soaking into the wall. It also has a decorative purpose—it is a way of finishing off the wall and making it pleasing to the eye.

OTHER STRUCTURES

Box structures
Plan the bond so that the bricks can be run from side to corner, and from corner to side, without being cut.

Arches
In garden brickwork, arches are best built either from half-bricks, or from bricks that run through the thickness of the wall. Either way, the bricks are placed so that the stretcher (side) or header (end) face of the brick is looking to the inside of the arch.

Columns and pillars
The simplest freestanding column or pillar can be merely a brick square, with the bricks turned 90° in neighboring courses, and each course showing either a stretcher or a pair of headers (opposite left). However, the best option is to go for a pillar that has a stretcher alongside a header in every course (opposite right).

ABOVE Whole bricks running on their stretcher face.

ABOVE A single-brick-thick wall with an arch made of half-bricks.

LEFT A minimal, two-by-two pillar for rough work.

LEFT A four-by-four pillar for top-quality work.

atios, paths, and steps

Patios, paths, and steps are an essential part of everyday life. If you need one of these structures for your garden, what better way of making it than by laying a pattern of bricks? Whether you are planning a minute patio outside the back door, a functional path running the length of the garden, or a very short decorative step up to the front door, bricks will do the job beautifully. Old bricks have a special character and charm.

CONSTRUCTING PATIOS AND PATHS

Patios

A patio always needs a footing to stop it sinking, and an edging to stop it spreading. These need to be equal (in size, structure, and permanence) to the composition of the soil, the character of the patio, the combined weight of the materials, and to the expected usage. A firm, dry, stony soil requires the minimum of groundwork, but a wet, soft site requires hardpan, concrete, and drainage, plus an edging complete with a footing.

Paths

Because a path gets heavier use than a patio, it needs a deeper footing and a more permanent edging. The stucture of the edging might need to change over its length depending on the character-istics of the garden that borders it (e.g lawn, flowerbed).

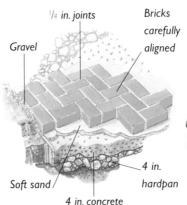
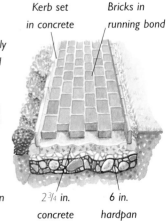

1/4 in. joints · Bricks carefully aligned · Gravel · Kerb set in concrete · Bricks in running bond · Soft sand · 4 in. hardpan · 4 in. concrete · 2 3/4 in. concrete · 6 in. hardpan

ABOVE A patio footing with formwork left in place.

ABOVE A path footing with extra depth of hardpan.

PATTERNS FOR PATIOS AND PATHS

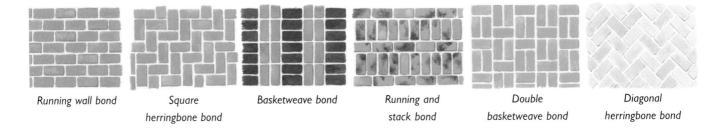

Running wall bond · Square herringbone bond · Basketweave bond · Running and stack bond · Double basketweave bond · Diagonal herringbone bond

CONSTRUCTING STEPS

Steps in the garden

The height (riser measurement) and width of a step are very important. Steps should be no greater than 9 in. high, and no less than 2 in. high (a good average would be 6 in.). The width of the tread should be at least 12–16 in. (front to back).

A single step on firm ground needs only a footing of compacted hardpan. If the soil is soft and you want three or more steps, the bottom tread must be built on a firm footing of 4 in. of compacted hardpan and 4 in. of concrete.

A doorstep gets a lot of use, and needs a firm footing of 4 in. of compacted hardpan and 4 in. of concrete.

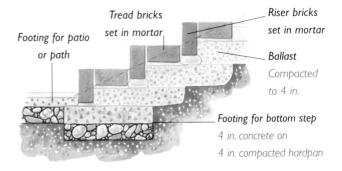

Footing for patio or path · Tread bricks set in mortar · Riser bricks set in mortar · Ballast Compacted to 4 in. · Footing for bottom step 4 in. concrete on 4 in. compacted hardpan

ABOVE If you want to ensure that the structure is extra-firm, replicate the footing for the bottom step under every step (do not use ballast).

Finishing and maintenance

It doesn't take long to transform a pile of bricks, a heap of sand, and lots of bags of portland cement into walls, paths, a patio, and other brick structures—all of which need to be finished off and cleaned. Occasionally, the brickwork will also need maintenance. This section shows you how. Remember that by keeping bricks free from plant growth and filling in cavities, you will help prevent frost damage.

CLEANING BRICKWORK AFTER BUILDING

Basic cleaning

If you take care, when laying bricks, not to splash, squirt, and smear mortar on the face of the brickwork, there should not be too much cleaning to do. Once the mortar has been left to dry overnight, use a stick of wood and a wire brush to knock off, and brush off, occasional splashes of mortar (concentrating on the brick and avoiding the mortar joints).

ABOVE Use a wire brush and work diagonally, so that you don't scour mortar out of the joints.

Chemical cleaning

Some types of brick can be cleaned with a special chemical that is sprayed or brushed on. This should be used only if recommended by the manufacturer of the bricks you are using, since it is possible to damage brickwork if used on the wrong type of brick.

Salts and efflorescence

A white powdery residue or "salting" may develop on the bricks, depending on type. This can be left, brushed off, or treated with vinegar or a chemical cleaner. On reconstituted stone (concrete products) such as block pavers or slabs, a patchy white effect may appear on the surface. This is normal and referred to as efflorescence. It is temporary but can be removed with special cleaners.

CLEANING: THINGS TO AVOID

- Do not touch mortar when it is still wet; leave overnight before cleaning.
- Do not let mortar become iron-hard before cleaning.
- Try not to wash away mortar from the joints.
- Do not scrape the surface of the bricks with metal tools.
- Avoid leaving a mortar residue when washing off the bricks.
- Do not use chemicals on brickwork unless recommended by the manufacturer.

MAINTAINING BRICKWORK

With brickwork projects, little or no maintenance is expected. Bricks should last several lifetimes; however, there are problems that may occur. Poor-quality bricks can crumble, frost can damage the surface of the bricks, or a brick may crack (cracks usually indicate poor pointing—see below for how to remedy). Mortar can be eroded quickly if the mortar mix was poorly measured out; erosion is also possible after many years, especially when exposed to lots of harsh, wet weather.

Repointing

Repointing is the process of replacing some of the mortar between the bricks, and is necessary when the original mortar has been eroded. Before adding slivers of new mortar, it may first be necessary to rake or chisel out mortar to make an adequate recess of about 1/2 in. deep. Experiment with a small area first, in order to ensure a good color match. Finish as you would for normal pointing (see page 27).

Replacing bricks

Find a new, matching brick, and use a brick chisel and a stonemason's hammer to cut out the damaged brick. Avoid damaging the surrounding bricks by levering with the chisel. Chisel out all the mortar in the recess and brush out the dust. Dampen the bottom and sides of the hole a little, prior to lining with stiff mortar. Put mortar on top of the replacement brick and carefully push it in place. Finish the joints as normal (see page 27).

Reinforcing brickwork

If brickwork in your garden is showing signs of structural failure, you will have to repair it. If the top of a wall is disintegrating, the top few courses need to be relaid and a protective coping added.

If brickwork is cracked or leaning, the footing is failing. If the problem doesn't look too bad, reinforce or underpin the footing, bit by bit, with sections of additional concrete, and replace the damaged brickwork. If the wall looks really dreadful, demolish it.

Part 2: **Projects**

Flower border edging

If your flower borders merge into the lawn, smarten them up with a neat brick edging. This traditional English design, commonly found in Sussex, uses rows of beautiful handmade bricks to form a decorative edge that separates the soil from the lawn. It looks very attractive, especially in a cottage garden. Brick edging is also a wonderful timesaver when it comes to mowing the lawn.

TIME

One weekend per 16 ft. length of edging.

SPECIAL TIPS

This design is intended for straight borders, but it can also be used for gentle curves (experiment without mortar before you build).

CUTAWAY DETAIL OF THE FLOWER BORDER EDGING

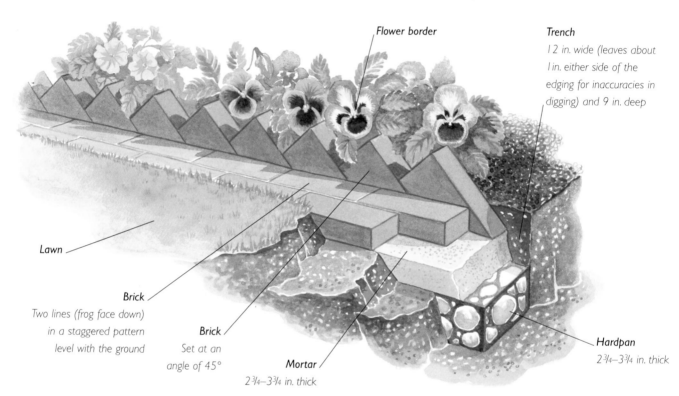

Flower border

Trench
12 in. wide (leaves about 1 in. either side of the edging for inaccuracies in digging) and 9 in. deep

Lawn

Brick
Two lines (frog face down) in a staggered pattern level with the ground

Brick
Set at an angle of 45°

Mortar
2¾–3¾ in. thick

Hardpan
2¾–3¾ in. thick

BORDER LINES

This design is very practical: the rows of bricks are laid at the same level as the lawn, making it easy to mow (and less work to trim). The lawnmower can be pushed hard up against the zigzag edging that holds back the soil, with its wheels running along the brick track next to it.

There are a number of options you may want to consider before starting. First of all, think about the style of your garden and whether or not this traditional English pattern is suitable. For a more modern look, for example, you could have a single line of black bricks partnered with a line of blue glazed tiles.

This is a very simple project to make and you are unlikely to encounter any problems. In fact, it is an ideal project to begin with if you are new to brickwork.

YOU WILL NEED

Materials *for an edging 16 ft. long and 10 in. wide*
- Bricks: 85
- Hardpan: 7 cu. feet
- Mortar: 1 part (80 lb.) portland cement and 4 parts (320 lb.) sand

Tools
- Tape measure, pegs, and string
- Spade and fork
- Wheelbarrow and bucket
- Sledgehammer
- Shovel and mixing board, or cement mixer
- Mason's trowel
- Stonemason's hammer
- Brick chisel

Step-by-step: Making the flower border edging

Digging
Dig out the soil in shallow spadefuls

Sod
Remove the sod first and see if it can be used elsewhere in the garden

String
Make sure that the two strings remain taut and parallel

 Decide where to put the edging (we wanted to increase the width of an existing flower border and avoid damaging plants). Use the pegs and string to mark an area 12 in. wide (this leaves about 1 in. either side of the edging for inaccuracies in digging) and as long as your border. Use the spade and fork to remove the sod and dig a trench 9 in. deep. Remove the pegs and string.

2 Spread hardpan in the trench and use the sledgehammer to compact it. Break up any pieces larger than half a brick. Continue spreading hardpan, breaking and compacting until you have filled the trench with 2¾–3¾ in. of hardpan. Remove any pieces that stick up above this height.

Hardpan
Systematically break and compact the hardpan until you have a level layer

Stonemason's hammer
Let the weight of the hammer do the work

Flower border
Remove the sod to extend the border when the edging is in place

3 Spread mortar along a 40 in.-long section of trench, using the bricklayer's trowel, making it 2¾–3¾ in. thick. Don't try to do more than 40 in. at a time. Position two lines of bricks (frog face down) in a staggered pattern and knock them level with the ground using the handle of the stonemason's hammer. Use the stonemason's hammer and brick chisel to cut half-bricks when needed.

Level
Try to keep the bricks level with each other (and slightly lower than the level of the lawn)

Guide
Use the width of a brick to ascertain the depth of the zigzag

4 Position the angled bricks carefully and tap them into the bed of mortar. Aim for an angle of 45°. You can use another brick as a guide to how far the brick needs to sink down (as shown); alternatively just knock it in so that it appears even. Finish the section; repeat the procedure to complete the edging.

Helpful hint

After placing about six angled bricks, stand back and check that they are all at 45° and pushed down to the correct depth. If things go wrong, just pull out the offending bricks, then add extra mortar and replace in the correct position.

Country cottage path

One of the best ways of creating a joyous splash of color and pattern in the garden

is to build a red brick path in the country cottage tradition. It's a beautifully simple

concept that involves gathering as many bricks as you can find—the older and more

battered the better—and arranging them in a three-by-three basketweave pattern.

YOU WILL NEED

Materials *for a path 13 ft. long
and about 4 ft. wide*
- Bricks: 173
- Hardpan: 8¾ cu. feet.
- Ballast: 550 lb.
- Sand: 550 lb.
- Mortar: 1 part (34 lb.)
  portland cement and 4 parts
  (136 lb.) sand
- Lumber: 26 ft. of 2 x 3 in.
  section (formwork),
  6 pieces (minimum), 12 in.
  long, 2 in. wide, and 1 in. thick
  (pegs), 1 piece, 27 in. long, 4
  in. wide, and 1 in. thick; 1
  piece, 30 in. long, 2 in. wide,
  and 1 in. thick (screed strip)

- Nails: 6 (minimum) x 2 in.
  (formwork), and 2 x 1 in.
  (screed strip)

Tools
- Tape measure, pegs,
  and string
- Stonemason's hammer
- Spade and fork
- Wheelbarrow and bucket
- Sledgehammer
- Handsaw
- Claw hammer
- Power tamper
- Shovel and mixing board, or
  cement mixer
- Mason's trowel
- Rake
- Broom

PAVING THE WAY

Many beautiful gardens feature patterned brickwork paths. The
warm tones of clay bricks arranged in small-scale, intricate
patterns look wonderful, especially on a hazy summer's day when
they are set against the fresh tones of foliage and a bright patchwork of flowers.

Various combinations of brick color and layout pattern offer
endless design possibilities. This basketweave design will look great
in traditional, cottage-type gardens. Most designs entail the same
building techniques as this path. The path is ideal for light use and
is just the right width to permit a wheelbarrow to be pushed
along it. If you need a wider path, let the pattern of bricks dictate
the precise width (and avoid cutting bricks as much as possible).

You won't be digging down too deep to make the footing, so
do not worry about exposing pipes leading to and from the
house; however, take the usual precautions when siting the path.
Check the location of underground utility pipes (gas, water main,
drains, oil supplies) and avoid situating a project nearby.

CUTAWAY DETAIL OF THE COUNTRY COTTAGE PATH

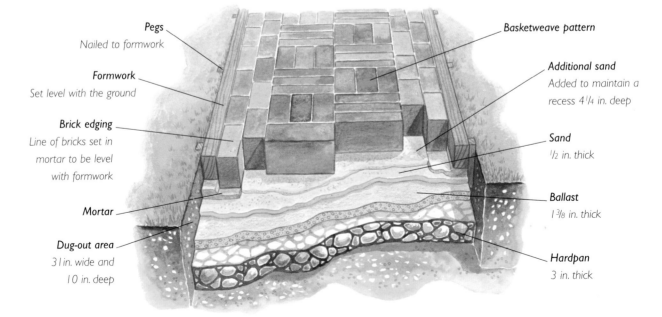

Pegs
Nailed to formwork

Formwork
Set level with the ground

Brick edging
*Line of bricks set in
mortar to be level
with formwork*

Mortar

Dug-out area
*31 in. wide and
10 in. deep*

Basketweave pattern

Additional sand
*Added to maintain a
recess 4¼ in. deep*

Sand
½ in. thick

Ballast
1⅜ in. thick

Hardpan
3 in. thick

Step-by-step: Making the country cottage path

Hardpan
Pound into small pieces
to form a compact layer

Screed strip
Use the board to spread
and level the ballast

Sledgehammer
Choose a
hammer weight
to suit your
strength

Path width
The space
between the
formwork
boards should
be 4 ft.

Pegs
Fixed to
outer side of
formwork

1 Plan where the path is to go and use the tape measure, stonemason's hammer, pegs, and string to mark out an area on the ground 32 in. wide and as long as required. Dig out the sod and soil to a depth of 10 in. using the spade and fork. Spread hardpan in the trench and pound it with a sledgehammer to break up large pieces and form a compacted, level layer 3 in. thick.

2 Nail pegs to the outer side of the formwork and position it in the trench so that it is level with the ground on either side. Test that your bricks fit within the formwork by laying out a small area of pattern. Spread ballast to just above the level of the bottom of the formwork and use the power tamper to compact it into a layer $1\frac{1}{2}$ in. thick. Make a screed strip and scrape away the excess ballast.

3 Mix up some stiff mortar and lay a line of bricks either side of the path, setting them on their stretcher face (side). Do not leave gaps between the bricks. Tap them level with the top of the formwork and use the trowel to scrape away the excess mortar that squeezes out from under the bricks.

Mortar
Scrape away
excess mortar

Edging
Set the bricks
level with the
formwork

Working action
Use a gentle tapping
and dragging action

Screed strip
Revise the size
of the strip to
allow for the
¹/₂ in. of
sand that has
been added

4 Once the mortar has set, spread a layer of sand and use the power tamper to compact it into a layer ¹/₂ in. thick. Avoid vibrating and dislodging the edge bricks. Spread more sand and revise the size of the screed strip so that it fits between the rows of edge bricks. Scrape away excess sand to leave a recess, about 4¹/₄ in. deep, for the rest of the bricks.

Depth
Check the
depth of the
recess—it needs
to be 4¹/₄ in.

Size and color
Experiment
to find the
most attractive
arrangement
of colors and
the best fit

5 Lay the bricks, stretcher face up, in the basketweave pattern. Avoid treading on the sand. Work from one end to the other and occasionally stand back to check your progress. When all the bricks have been laid, brush sand into the joints. Fix a pad (or piece of carpet) to the power tamper and run it over the bricks.

Helpful hint

Because bricks are proportioned to allow for the mortar joints used in bricklaying, the gaps between the bricks at the sides and ends will vary. Compensate for this by distributing them as evenly as possible.

Raised herringbone patio

The wonderful thing about a patio is that it immediately becomes a focal point, and broadens the way you use the garden. It makes a great surface for a barbecue, the perfect place for a family meal, and a safe area for children to play on. If you enjoy doing puzzles, you will like the process of laying the herringbone surface.

CUTAWAY DETAIL OF THE
RAISED HERRINGBONE PATIO

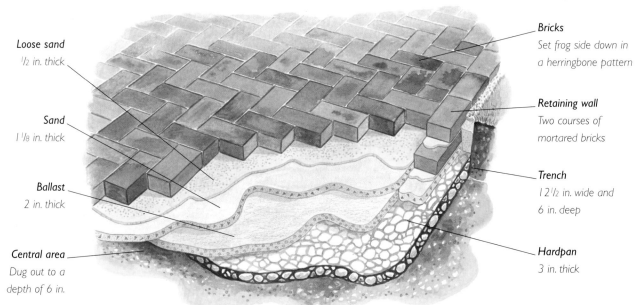

Loose sand
1/2 in. thick

Sand
1 1/8 in. thick

Ballast
2 in. thick

Central area
Dug out to a depth of 6 in.

Bricks
Set frog side down in a herringbone pattern

Retaining wall
Two courses of mortared bricks

Trench
12 1/2 in. wide and 6 in. deep

Hardpan
3 in. thick

YOU WILL NEED

Materials *for a patio about 10 ft. square*
- Bricks: 104 (retaining wall) and 351 (patio surface)
- Hardpan: 26.5 cu. feet
- Ballast: 1.1 tons
- Sand: 1.1 tons
- Mortar: 1 part (44 lb.) portland cement and 4 parts (176 lb.) sand
- Wood: 1 piece, 10 ft. long, 6 in. wide, and 1 in. thick (screed strip)

Tools
- Tape measure, pegs, and string
- Stonemason's hammer
- Spade and fork
- Wheelbarrow and bucket
- Sledgehammer
- Shovel and mixing board, or cement mixer
- Mason's trowel and pointing trowel
- Level
- Power tamper
- Rake
- Brick chisel
- Broom

A PATTERN TO FOLLOW

If you have a small, modern yard, you can adjust this design to make it less quaint—perhaps by inserting contrasting zigzags of stone, inlaid wood or textured metal. Or a variation in the pattern might appeal (see pages 28 and 30), but bear in mind that some patterns require many more bricks to be cut and therefore it will take longer to make the patio.

This concept of a raised patio built within a retaining wall is often chosen in order to minimize the building work involved in a patio project, because less soil needs digging and removing from the site than for a ground-level patio. Even so, remember that building any patio is hard work, and fairly costly because you are usually dealing with a large area. Save up for quality bricks, allocate a few weekends to complete the work, and enlist some help.

When surveying your site, consider the finished height of the patio in relation to existing doorways, steps or paths. If the patio is to be attached to the house, do not cover air bricks (perforated bricks near the bottom of the walls of the house) and do not build the patio any higher than 6 in. below the damp course of the house. Most importantly, the patio should slope away from the house by 1 in. per 6 ft.

Step-by-step: **Making the raised herringbone patio**

Trench
Dig out to 12½ in. wide
and 6 in. deep

Hardpan
Compact the
hardpan until it
is level and
3 in. thick

Level
Remove stubborn
pieces that
stand proud

1 Using the tape measure, pegs, string, and stonemason's hammer, mark out the size and position of the patio, leaving an extra 4 in. all around (just over 10 ft. square). If you are building against a wall, do not add on an extra 4 in. on that side. Check that the patio area is square (see page 21). Dig a trench (12½ in. wide and 6 in. deep) all around the edge, within the square. Spread hardpan in the trench and compact with the sledgehammer to a finished depth of 3 in.

Stonemason's
hammer
Use the
handle of
the hammer
to knock
the bricks
into position

Wall
Build the wall
two bricks high.
On the top
course, lay the frog
face downward

2 Build a two-brick-high retaining wall along the middle of the trench. Lay the first course of bricks on a generous thickness of mortar, leaving ¼ in.-wide joints between the bricks. Check that the wall is straight and level (or sloping away from your house as appropriate). Finish the joints with the pointing trowel (by inserting mortar if necessary, smoothing, scraping away, and creating a slight dip between the edges of adjoining bricks). Lay the second course with the frog face downward.

Wall
Top course of the wall forms the edging

Power tamper
A safe, easy-to-use machine

3 While you are waiting for the mortar to set, dig out the central area within the wall to a depth of 6 in. Spread a layer of hardpan and using the sledgehammer, break and compact it to a depth of 3 in. Spread a thick layer of ballast and compact it with the power tamper until 2 in. deep, followed by a layer of sand compacted to a depth of 1¼ in. Prepare a 10 ft.-long screed strip by cutting a 2¼ in. (brick height) x 4¼ in. notch out of both ends. Ask someone to hold the other end and scrape off excess sand by dragging the strip across the patio area while the notched ends are engaged with the brick wall.

Bricks
Arrange bricks (frog side down) for best fit and color effect

4 Fill low areas with more sand and compact again. Screed once more and then rake ½ in. of loose sand over the whole area. Lay the bricks in a herringbone pattern. Using the brick chisel and stonemason's hammer, cut bricks to fill the small gaps. Sweep sand into the joints. Fix a pad (or piece of carpet) to the power tamper and run the machine over the bricks.

Helpful hint

Aim for even gaps between the bricks; stand back every now and then to check your progress. For areas larger than 10 ft. square, use a string line as a guide to laying the bricks in a straight line.

Classic birdbath

A birdbath must surely be one of the most decorative and interesting things to have in a garden. If you enjoy watching birds splashing the hours away, try building this straightforward pillar, which is topped with a ready-made birdbath. Site it so that it can be viewed from a patio, or the house, for year-round entertainment value.

TIME

Half a day to make th
footing and four day
to build the pillar.

SPECIAL TIPS

This structure can
also be used for
mounting a sundial.

YOU WILL NEED

Materials *for a pillar about 3.5 ft. high and 22 in. square*
- Bricks: 82
- Tiles: 36 tiles, 5.5 in. square and ½ in. thick
- Paving slab: 17 in. square and 1½ in. thick
- Hardpan: 3½ cu. feet
- Concrete: 1 part (88 lb.) portland cement and 4 parts (352 lb.) ballast
- Mortar: 1 part (28 lb.) portland cement and 4 parts (112 lb.) sand
- Wood: 4 pieces, 28 in. long, 5 in. wide, and 2 in. thick (formwork),
  4 pieces, 15 in. long, 3 in. wide, and 2 in. thick (collar)
- Nails: 16 x 3 in.
- Birdbath dish: 14 in. square and 3.5 in. high

Tools
- Tape measure and piece of chalk
- Handsaw
- Claw hammer
- Spade
- Wheelbarrow and bucket
- Sledgehammer
- Level
- Shovel and mixing board, or cement mixer
- Mason's trowel and pointing trowel
- Brick chisel
- Rubber mallet
- Tile cutter

A FASCINATING VIEW

Most of us enjoy watching birds in the garden, and a birdbath will help to attract them. This restrained, architectural-looking design also has other possibilities. Without the birdbath on top, the pillar can make a dramatic plinth for a classical statuette. (Fix the statue to the top with a 12 in.-long steel rod in. in diameter. Drill a hole in the top of the pillar (⅜ in. in diameter) with a masonry bit, making it at least 6 in. deep. Drill a 6 in.-deep hole in the statue. Drop the rod into the pillar and put the statue on top. The rod will stop the statue being blown off or knocked off.) The pillar could also form the base for a sundial.

Personalize the design by choosing a birdbath handmade from metal, stone, or wood, or a decorative shallow ceramic pot. The tile details could also be altered—perhaps a line of tiles on every course, or thick black slate substituted instead. Decorative patterned tiles could also be inserted into the brickwork.

EXPLODED VIEW OF THE CLASSIC BIRDBATH

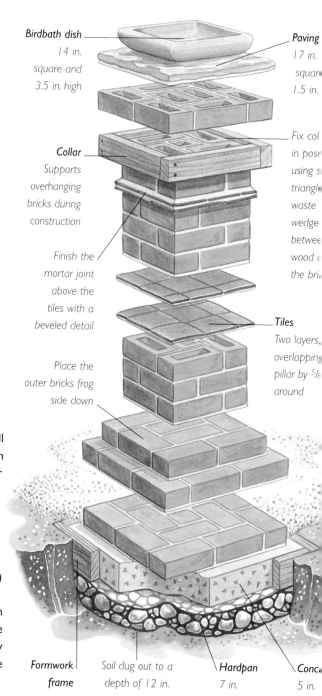

Birdbath dish
14 in.
square and
3.5 in. high

Paving
17 in.
squar
1.5 in.

Fix col
in posi
using s
triangle
waste
wedge
betwee
wood a
the bri

Collar
Supports
overhanging
bricks during
construction

Finish the
mortar joint
above the
tiles with a
beveled detail

Tiles
Two layers,
overlappin
pillar by 5⁄
around

Place the
outer bricks frog
side down

Formwork
frame

Soil dug out to a
depth of 12 in.

Hardpan
7 in.

Conc
5 in.

Step-by-step: Making the classic birdbath

Edging bricks
Place these bricks with the frog face downward

Center bricks
Arrange the inner bricks with frog face uppermost

1 Make the formwork frame using two 3 in. nails at each corner. Lay the frame on the ground and roughly mark around it with the spade. Put the frame aside and dig out the marked soil to a depth of 12 in. Fill the area with hardpan and compact it to a thickness of 7 in. with the sledgehammer. Lay the frame on top and make sure that it is level, then fill with concrete. When the concrete is dry, practice laying the first course of bricks.

Rubber mallet
Using this avoids damaging the bricks

Third course
Bricks placed frog face down

Level
Make sure all the bricks are bedded to the same level. Note that the outer bricks are used frog side down

Joints
Note the staggered arrangement of the vertical joints

Pointing
Use the pointing trowel to point the joints

2 Chalk around the bricks. Remove them and spread mortar within the marks. Lay the first course and ensure that it is level and square by checking the side and diagonal measurements (see page 21). Lay the second course in the same way, but with the vertical joints staggered.

3 Clean up the joints of the first two courses. Practice laying the third course, which is stepped inward. Mark its position with chalk, and lay the bricks on a bed of mortar. Repeat for the fourth course. Continue building up to the level of the tiles and leave the pillar overnight.

Leveling
Sandwich and bed the tiles
in mortar and tap level

4 Cut and fit two layers of tiles to cover the area, allowing an overlap of $5/8$ in. all around the pillar. Make sure that none of the joints coincide. The tiles can be quite tricky to lay neatly, so work slowly and carefully. Use the level to check that they are level.

Tiles
Cut and fit the tiles so that they overhang by $5/8$ in.

Mortar
Rake out a little of the mortar between the tiles

Wooden collar
Make a frame that fits loosely around the top of the pillar and wedge it in place with small triangles of waste wood so that it cannot move. The collar will support the weight of the overhanging bricks. (When the project is complete, wait 48 hours before removing the collar)

5 Continue building up the courses of brick and tile that create the pillar, checking that each course is level and the corners remain vertical. Make the wooden collar to support the final overhanging layer of bricks and wedge it in place. Build the final course of bricks. Position the slab and clean up the joints. Place the birdbath dish on top.

Helpful hint

Positioning the collar is difficult to do on your own, so ask somebody to help. If the collar keeps slipping down or going crooked, try using differently shaped wedges, and more of them.

.lanted patio

Just imagine a warm summer's evening, when you can sit outside enjoying the stored heat given off by the patio, and wafts of scent from surrounding plants. This patio design incorporates beds of soil, which have been planted with a selection of herbs. Concrete paving blocks, bricks, or clay paving blocks can be used for the paving.

TIME

Five days to prepare the footing and two days to lay the blocks.

SPECIAL TIPS

If you want a different pattern of blocks, experiment by arranging them on the ground.

YOU WILL NEED

Materials *for a planted patio about 16 ft. square*
- Concrete paving blocks: 714 blocks, 8 in. long, 4 in. wide, and 2 in. thick (or bricks or clay paving blocks—if using these, adjust quantity, overall patio measurements, and depth of footing)
- Hardpan: 88 cu. feet.
- Concrete: 1 part (0.55 tons) portland cement and 4 parts (2.2 tons) ballast
- Mortar: 1 part (165 lb.) portland cement and 4 parts (660 lb.) sand
- Wood: 92 ft. of 6 x 1 in. section (formwork), 56 pieces, 12 in. long, 1.5 in. wide, and 1 in. thick (formwork pegs), and 1 piece, 5.5 ft. long,

4 in. wide, and 1 in. thick (tamping board)
- Nails: 172 x 1.5 in.

Tools
- Tape measure, pegs, and string
- Spade and fork
- Wheelbarrow and bucket
- Handsaw
- Claw hammer
- Level
- Stonemason's hammer
- Sledgehammer
- Shovel and mixing board, or cement mixer
- Brick chisel
- Pointing trowel
- Gardener's trowel

SETTING THE STYLE

This design offers a blend of planting and paving reminiscent of a medieval herb garden. It can be enjoyed as a pathway through a miniature landscape, or somewhere to sit in peace on your own, or as a place to savor the fragrance of herbs. If you wish, you can change the balance of planting to paving, or move the planting to one side and have a larger paved area for sitting.

Patios require a big investment in time and materials, so make sure that you can manage a project of this size. You shouldn't come across any pipes while digging the footing, because it isn't very deep, but always be cautious and get advice if you uncover pipes that you were not expecting. The major part of the work is the digging and the setting out of the wooden formwork, so don't be dismayed if things seem slow at first.

CUTAWAY VIEW OF
THE PLANTED PATIO

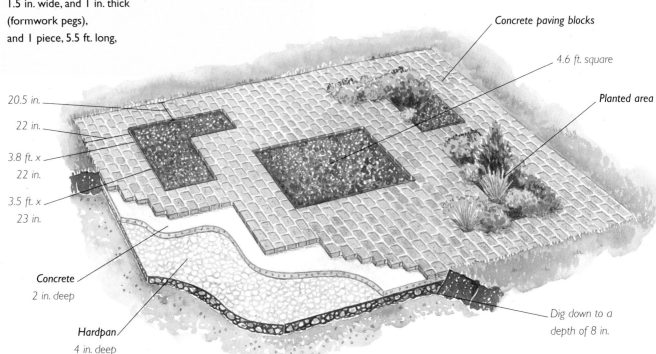

Concrete paving blocks

4.6 ft. square

Planted area

20.5 in.

22 in.

3.8 ft. x
22 in.

3.5 ft. x
23 in.

Concrete
2 in. deep

Hardpan
4 in. deep

Dig down to a
depth of 8 in.

Step-by-step: Making the planted patio

Hardpan
*Compact to a depth of 4 in. and
1 1/8 – 1 1/2 in. lower than the formwork*

Formwork
*Build formwork
frames using
two nails at
each corner.
Nail pegs to
the inside of
the frames*

1 Dig out a level area of soil 16 ft. square and 8 in. deep. Mark out the paved and planted areas with pegs and string. Make up formwork frames to the size and shape of the planting areas. Knock these into the ground so that they are level with each other. Spread hardpan where the paving will be, and compact it to a depth of 4 in.

Helpful hint

You will get a slightly better result if you can leave a gap between the hardpan and the formwork. With this method, the concrete will form a stronger edge around the planting areas.

Concrete
*Should have a
crumbly texture*

2 Mix up some concrete using very little water (it should be crumbly), and shovel it over the hardpan. Use the tamping board to tamp the concrete level with the top of the formwork. It is possible to work on your own, but the task is much easier if you have help. Either way, do not tread on the concrete, and do not try to build more than a quarter of the patio in one go.

Tamping
*Tamp the
concrete level
with the top of
the formwork*

Bedding
Dampen the underside of the bricks and wiggle into place

String line
Use a taut string line as a guide

3 Without waiting for the concrete to dry, set up a string line to indicate where to lay the first line of blocks and gently bed each block, leaving gaps of about $1/2$ in. between them. The concrete is already level, so there is no need to tap the blocks down or check levels—just wiggle them into position and occasionally stand back to check your lines are straight and gaps are equal.

Joints
Aim for joints that are about $1/2$ in. wide

Mortar
Push crumbly mortar into the joints

Formwork
Remove the formwork and fill with soil

Pointing
Use the handle of the pointing trowel to smooth and finish the joints

Soil
Use a planting mixture to suit your plants

Plants
Choose plants carefully. Before planting, lay them out in their pots to look at the pattern you are creating. Take into account their size when fully grown.

4 Use a brick chisel and stonemason's hammer to cut blocks to fill in small spaces. Mix up some mortar using very little water (like the concrete, it should be crumbly) and scrape this into the gaps. Push it down into the gaps until you have filled the full depth. Finish the joints.

5 Leave the concrete and mortar to set fully (or wait at least two days) and then clean up any excess mortar. Remove the formwork and loosen the soil in the planting areas with the fork, and top them up with good soil or compost to the level of the bricks.

Inspirations: Brick patios

While patios made from concrete, reconstituted stone slabs, or tarmac can be overpowering and visually intrusive, brick patios somehow seem to blend into their surroundings much better. A well-built brick patio looks charming, solid, and imposing—perfect for just about everything from a cottage to a townhouse. The bricks can be laid in all sorts of patterns to create attractive designs, possibly incorporating different-colored bricks or other materials.

ABOVE **A** patio made from local bricks, seashore cobblestones, and field flints. The owner wanted to create an unexpected retreat in a secluded part of the garden, and chose a semicircle outlined by pebbles to create an unusual, decorative shape.

ABOVE **This sizeable stone and brick patio forms a practical and attractive surface around a farmhouse. The brickwork infill echoes the walls of the house, ensuring that the house and patio complement each other.**

LEFT **A huge brick patio that encircles a low dwarf hedge and looks rather like a very wide path. The patio is built to accommodate a sloping site—the outer edge is raised and the inner edge is flush with the turf by the hedge.**

Decorative raised bed

Raised beds are a good idea: not only do they give you the chance to increase the planting area in your garden, but better still—especially if you find it difficult to bend—they bring the garden up to a more manageable height and make it very easy to tend the plants. A raised bed can make a very suitable home for rockery plants, enabling you to enjoy these miniature plants at close quarters.

CROSS-SECTION OF THE DECORATIVE RAISED BED

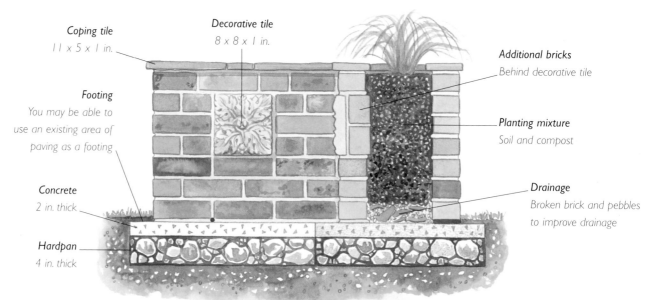

Coping tile
11 x 5 x 1 in.

Decorative tile
8 x 8 x 1 in.

Additional bricks
Behind decorative tile

Footing
You may be able to use an existing area of paving as a footing

Planting mixture
Soil and compost

Concrete
2 in. thick

Drainage
Broken brick and pebbles to improve drainage

Hardpan
4 in. thick

YOU WILL NEED

Materials *for a raised bed about 5 ft. x 5 ft. minus square section to create L-shape, and 22 in. high*
- Bricks: 128
- Decorative tiles: 2 tiles, 8 in. square and 1 in. thick
- Coping tiles: 14 tiles, 11 in. long, 5 in. wide, and 1 in. thick
- Mortar: 1 part (33 lb.) portland cement and 4 parts (132 lb.) sand

Tools
- Tape measure, long rule about 4 ft. long, and a piece of chalk
- Shovel and mixing board, or cement mixer
- Bricklayer's trowel and pointing trowel
- Level
- Brick hammer
- Brick chisel
- Stonemason's hammer
- Circular saw with masonry blade (may be required to cut the coping tiles)

RAISING THE STANDARDS

As with most projects, there are options and variations you might prefer instead of building exactly to the given specifications. If you are thinking about altering the size, remember that the size and shape of the bed both need careful consideration—it is tempting to build a bigger structure, but there is a danger of creating something that requires a massive amount of soil. This narrow corner design is great for small plants and doesn't need tons of soil to fill it. The decorative tiles make the building procedure more complicated, but are worth the extra trouble.

If you want to change the appearance of the raised bed, don't settle for boring materials until you have scoured the salvage yards for great-looking terra-cotta details or old-style patterned tiles. Brightly colored Victorian glazed tiles with floral designs will look wonderful set against the warm colors of the brick. You may also want to consider using contrasting colors of brick in lines or patterns, as used in the Storage Seat project on page 68.

Decorative raised bed

PLAN VIEW SHOWING THE FIRST COURSE OF BRICKS

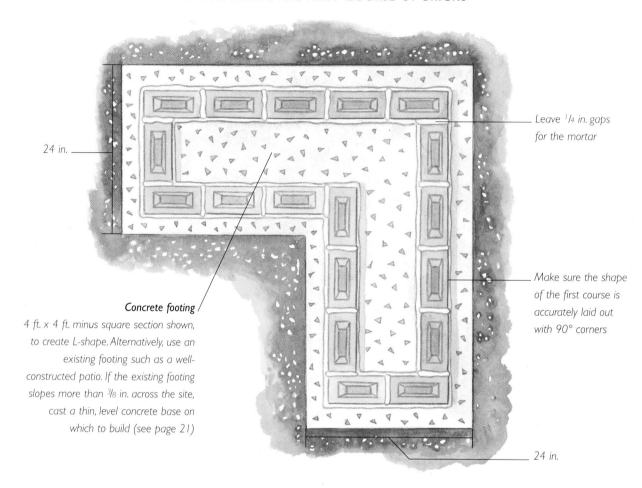

24 in.

Leave ¹/₄ in. gaps
for the mortar

Make sure the shape
of the first course is
accurately laid out
with 90° corners

Concrete footing

4 ft. x 4 ft. minus square section shown,
to create L-shape. Alternatively, use an
existing footing such as a well-
constructed patio. If the existing footing
slopes more than ³/₈ in. across the site,
cast a thin, level concrete base on
which to build (see page 21)

24 in.

DETAIL SHOWING THE RECESS FOR THE DECORATIVE TILE

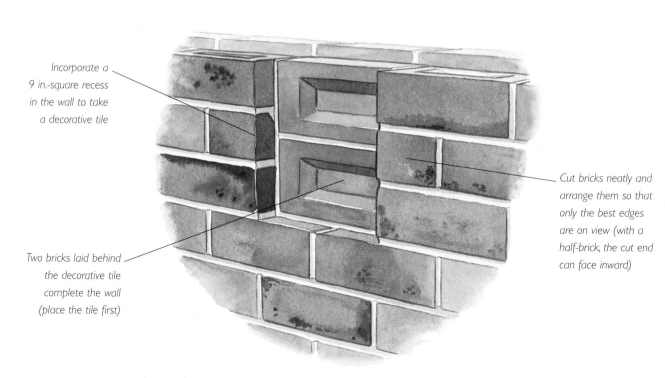

Incorporate a
9 in.-square recess
in the wall to take
a decorative tile

Cut bricks neatly and
arrange them so that
only the best edges
are on view (with a
half-brick, the cut end
can face inward)

Two bricks laid behind
the decorative tile
complete the wall
(place the tile first)

EXPLODED VIEW OF THE DECORATIVE RAISED BED

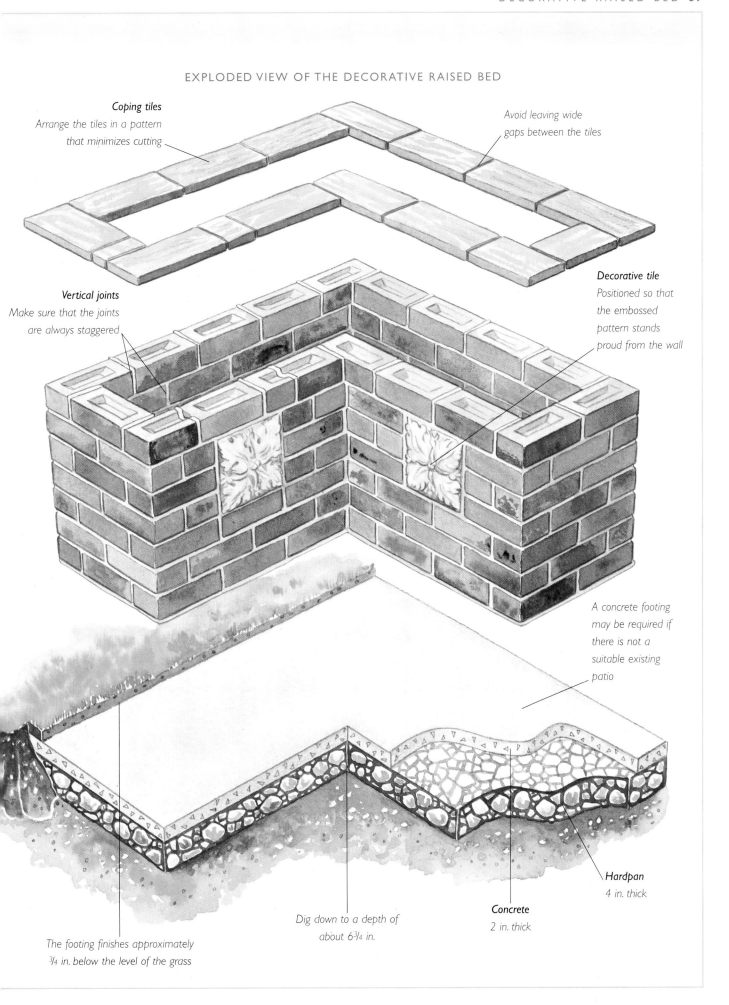

Coping tiles
Arrange the tiles in a pattern that minimizes cutting

Avoid leaving wide gaps between the tiles

Vertical joints
Make sure that the joints are always staggered

Decorative tile
Positioned so that the embossed pattern stands proud from the wall

A concrete footing may be required if there is not a suitable existing patio

The footing finishes approximately ¾ in. below the level of the grass

Dig down to a depth of about 6¾ in.

Concrete
2 in. thick

Hardpan
4 in. thick

Step-by-step: **Making the decorative raised bed**

Marking out
Use a piece of chalk and a long rule to mark out the shape

Corners
Check that the bricks form 90° corners

First course
Arrange the bricks in the correct position, leaving ¹/₄ in. gaps in between

Leveling
Use the level to help position the bricks accurately

Straight sides
Check that the bricks are in straight lines using the edge of the level

1 Work out where you would like the bed. We have put it on the corner of a patio that has a footing sufficiently adequate to support the additional weight of a raised bed. See pages 20–21 if you need to build a footing. Practice arranging the first course of bricks to establish the size and shape of the bed, and use the tape measure, chalk, and long rule to mark around them.

2 Lay the first course of bricks on a bed of mortar. Use the level to check that the bricks are accurately placed and stand back to scrutinize your work. The overall shape should have 90° corners, the sides should be straight, and the gaps between the bricks should be equal.

3 Lay a further two courses, making sure that each one is level and the vertical joints occur in the correct staggered positions. Clean up the joints using the pointing trowel.

Pointing
Use the pointing trowel to scrape away the excess mortar and smooth the joints between the bricks

Joints inside wall
Don't worry too much about the appearance of the mortar joints inside the structure— just scrape out the excess

Bricks
Use two bricks to weigh down the piece of wood that holds the tile in place

Decorative tile
Check that it is positioned centrally and vertically within the space, and that the pattern stands proud of the bricks

4 Build the next three courses, leaving square spaces in the front-facing walls to receive the decorative tiles. Spread mortar in these spaces and position the tiles. Hold each tile in position by placing a piece of wood across the top of the walls and weighting it with a couple of bricks. Put bricks behind the tile to support it (see hint).

Helpful hint

Wait for the mortar fixing the bricks to dry, then stack bricks inside the space behind the tile, and use a wooden prop to push the tile against the pile of bricks.

Level
Use the edge of the level to help you position the coping tiles in a straight line

5 Complete the last course of bricks. Note how the bricks in this course are cut (using the brick hammer) and arranged so that the joints do not coincide with the edges of the tile below (see main picture). Practice arranging the coping tiles in a pattern that minimizes cutting. Use the brick chisel and stonemason's hammer, or circular saw with masonry blade, to cut tiles. Bed the coping tiles on $1/4$ in. of mortar, using the side of the level to help align the edges of the tiles.

Simple garden wall

There is something very enjoyable about building a simple brick wall—the process of troweling slices of soft, smooth mortar, and placing one brick upon another, is a great escape from everyday worries. This freestanding low wall is suitable for a front garden wall, a wall around a raised patio, or a retaining wall for a small flower border. Or perhaps you have an unstable wall with missing bricks, which needs replacing.

TIME

Three days for a
10 ft. length of wall.

SAFETY

If you want a bigger wall,
see page 29 for details on
wall size and safety.

CROSS-SECTION DETAIL OF THE SIMPLE GARDEN WALL

Coping bricks

Bricks
*Laid in normal
stretcher bond*

Concrete
3½ in. thick

Hardpan
3½ in. thick

Tiles
*Two layers of
decorative tiles
help the wall
shed rainwater*

Soldier bricks
*Headers (ends)
facing forward*

*You may be able
to use an existing
footing such as a
strongly built patio*

YOU WILL NEED

Materials *for a wall
10 ft. long and 20 in. high*
- Bricks: 180
- Tiles: 36 tiles, 10 in. long,
  7 in. wide, and 0.5 in. thick
- Mortar: 1 part (55 lb.)
  portland cement and 4 parts
  (220 lb.) sand
- Wood: 1 piece, 10 ft. long,
  4 in. wide and 1 in. thick
  (leveling board)

Tools
- Shovel and mixing board, or
  cement mixer
- Wheelbarrow and bucket
- Bricklayer's trowel and
  pointing trowel
- Level
- Brick hammer

THE GREAT DIVIDE

A two-brick-thick wall is a good choice for most garden walls and will look better and last longer than the single-brick alternative. The pattern of bricks used in this wall is a traditional arrangement, and the layers of protruding tiles and beveled mortar detail are not just for decoration—to some extent they also protect the structure from water erosion. If you are contemplating a higher wall, you will need extra support (see page 29 on Supporting Piers and Buttresses) and you would certainly need a more substantial footing. For a wall that is twice as high, increase the size of the concrete footing slab to three times the width of the wall, and increase the thickness of the slab by 1⅛ in. A beginner should not attempt to build a wall higher than about 6 ft.

This low wall is built on an existing footing (see page 21 for how to assess suitability). See page 29 for how to build curved walls, change angles, and build around corners.

Simple garden wall

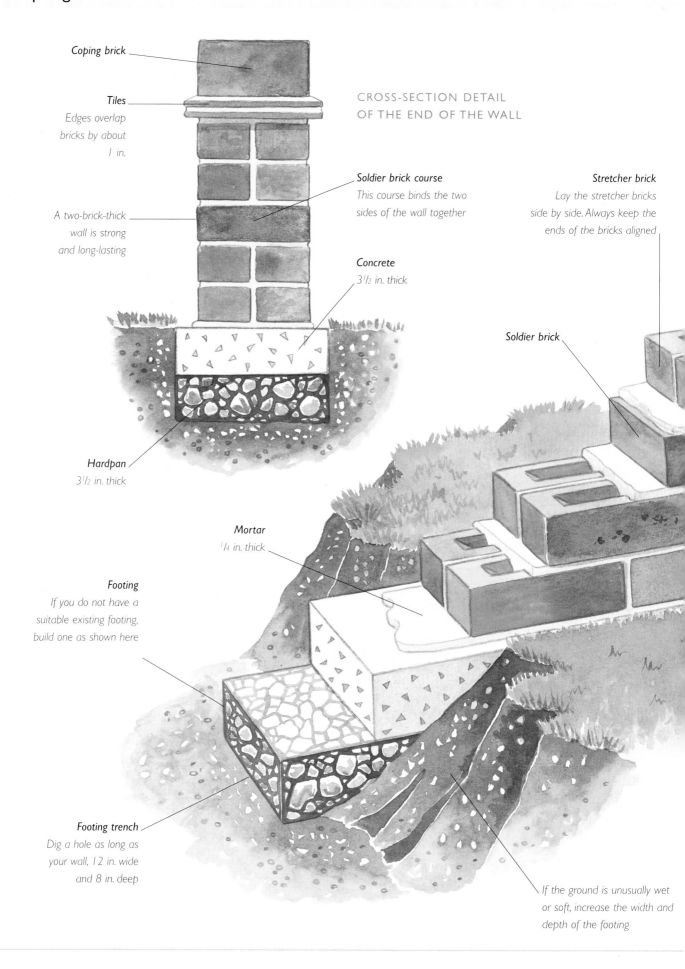

Coping brick

Tiles
*Edges overlap
bricks by about
1 in.*

*A two-brick-thick
wall is strong
and long-lasting*

CROSS-SECTION DETAIL
OF THE END OF THE WALL

Soldier brick course
*This course binds the two
sides of the wall together*

Concrete
3½ in. thick

Hardpan
3½ in. thick

Stretcher brick
*Lay the stretcher bricks
side by side. Always keep the
ends of the bricks aligned*

Soldier brick

Mortar
¼ in. thick

Footing
*If you do not have a
suitable existing footing,
build one as shown here*

Footing trench
*Dig a hole as long as
your wall, 12 in. wide
and 8 in. deep*

*If the ground is unusually wet
or soft, increase the width and
depth of the footing*

CUTAWAY DETAIL OF THE SIMPLE GARDEN WALL

Coping brick

Tile

*Arrange the tiles so that
the joints are staggered*

Coping brick

Mortar
$^1/_4$ in. thick

DETAIL OF THE MORTAR
JOINT AROUND THE TILES

Sloped mortar

*Shape and smooth the mortar to make
a sloped surface, triangular in section*

Tile

*If the tiles are slightly curved, lay
them so that the convex (dished)
surfaces face each other*

Step-by-step: Making the simple garden wall

First course
*Bed pairs of
bricks on mortar*

Leveling
*Use the leveling board
and level*

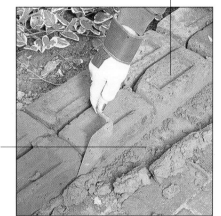

Footing
*In this instance,
there is a good,
solid footing
under the patio*

Cleaning up
*Wait until the
mortar has
partly dried,
then clean
it up*

Bond
*Build two
courses of
stretcher bond*

1 If there is a suitable footing (see page 21), you can start laying the bricks. Lay the first course of bricks on a generous bed of mortar. The bricks in each row should be equally spaced (3/8 in. joints) and placed exactly opposite each other. Check that the bricks are level and make adjustments as necessary.

2 Continue building the wall, this time staggering the joints of the second course so that they occur halfway along the bricks of the first course. Check the course is horizontal using the leveling board and the level. (At this point, you could also use a line set to help you, which establishes a level and a straight line, and is usually employed in the construction of long walls and houses—see page 12.)

Aligning
*Use the handle
of the hammer
to tap the
bricks into line*

3 The third course is of soldier bricks, with the headers (ends) of the bricks facing forward. In this course, alternate bricks should be centered on a joint underneath. Use the level to check that the wall is vertical, and make any necessary corrections by gently tapping bricks into line using the handle of the brick hammer. Build the fourth and fifth courses as for the first and second courses.

Third course
*Lay the soldier
brick course,
centering every
other brick
on the vertical
joints in
the course
underneath*

Tile position
Arrange the tiles so that there is an equal overhang at each side

Tile joints
Sandwich the tiles so that the joints are staggered

4 Lay the tiles on a ⅜ in.-thick bed of mortar, and avoid leaving any gaps in between them. Complete the first layer and proceed to the next. Start the second layer with half a tile (break with the brick hammer) so that the joints between the rows of tiles are staggered.

Helpful hint

The shape and texture of the tiles will affect the appearance of the wall. Do not use concrete tiles (the edges are not decorative) or tiles that are very curved or smooth—both can be troublesome to work with.

Coping bricks
Bedded on their stretcher face

Pointing
Point the top joints so that they are smooth and flush

Frogs
Should all face in the same direction

Mortar
Angle the mortar down to the edge of the tiles

Protection
The idea of the coping bricks and tiles is that they make rain run off without touching the wall

5 Spread mortar along the top of the wall and lay the coping bricks on their stretcher face (side), with all the frogs facing in the same direction. Finish with the frog of the last brick facing inward (so that the frog is not visible). Check that the coping is straight and level.

6 Clean up all the joints that still need doing and then concentrate on the mortar detail above the line of tiles. Spread mortar along the join and smooth it to form a sloped surface that is triangular in section (see drawing).

Storage seat

If your shed is bulging at the seams, this useful storage seat will provide a practical and attractive solution. It also gives you the opportunity to build a decorative brick box in the English diaper tradition (an allover surface decoration of a small repeated pattern such as diamonds or squares, using colored, projecting, or recessed bricks).

TIME
Three days if using an existing footing.

SPECIAL TIPS
The seat is heavy. You may want to consider a hinged design.

YOU WILL NEED

Materials *for a storage seat about 4.5 ft. long, 26 in. wide, and 20 in. high*
- Bricks: 67 light-colored bricks and 23 dark-colored bricks
- Mortar: 1 part (22 lb.) portland cement and 4 parts (88 lb.) sand
- Wood: 2 pieces, 4.5 ft. long, 2.5 in. wide, and 1.5 in. thick; and 6 pieces, 23 in. long, 2.5 in. wide, and 1.5 in. thick (seat frame), 6 pieces, 4.5 ft. long, 4 in. wide, and 1 in. thick (seat planks)

- Plywood (exterior grade): 1 piece, 4.5 ft. long, 26 in. wide, and ¼ in. thick (underseat board)
- Nails: 16 x 4 in. (frame) and 36 x 2 in. (seat planks)

Tools
- Tape measure and a piece of chalk
- Shovel and mixing board, or cement mixer
- Wheelbarrow and bucket
- Mason's trowel and pointing trowel
- Level
- Brick hammer
- Handsaw
- Claw hammer

ON THE BENCH

Have you ever looked at a plastic storage chest and thought that it would be really useful for the garden, but decided that it was far too ugly? Well, if you like good-looking, hard-working garden structures, this project might appeal to you. We have built the storage seat on the edge of a patio, where it can be used to hide away tools, pots, and other paraphernalia, keeping them protected from the weather. The slatted seat is made from preserved pine, with an underseat board of exterior plywood beneath the slats to stop rain getting into the storage space. Oak slats would look even better, but are more expensive. If you don't need storage space and just want a seat, you could make a lower structure and fashion the seat out of chunky railroad ties. The diamond pattern of dark bricks is not difficult to achieve and can be altered if you want a different effect. Bands of different-colored bricks, contrasting corner bricks, terra-cotta tiles, and glazed tiles are some of the options open to you.

FRONT VIEW OF THE STORAGE SEAT

Wooden seat
Protects contents from getting wet.
Lifts off completel

Light-colored bricks

Build a footing like this or use an existing footing

Dark-colored bricks
Use contrasting bricks for the pattern and the first course

Storage seat

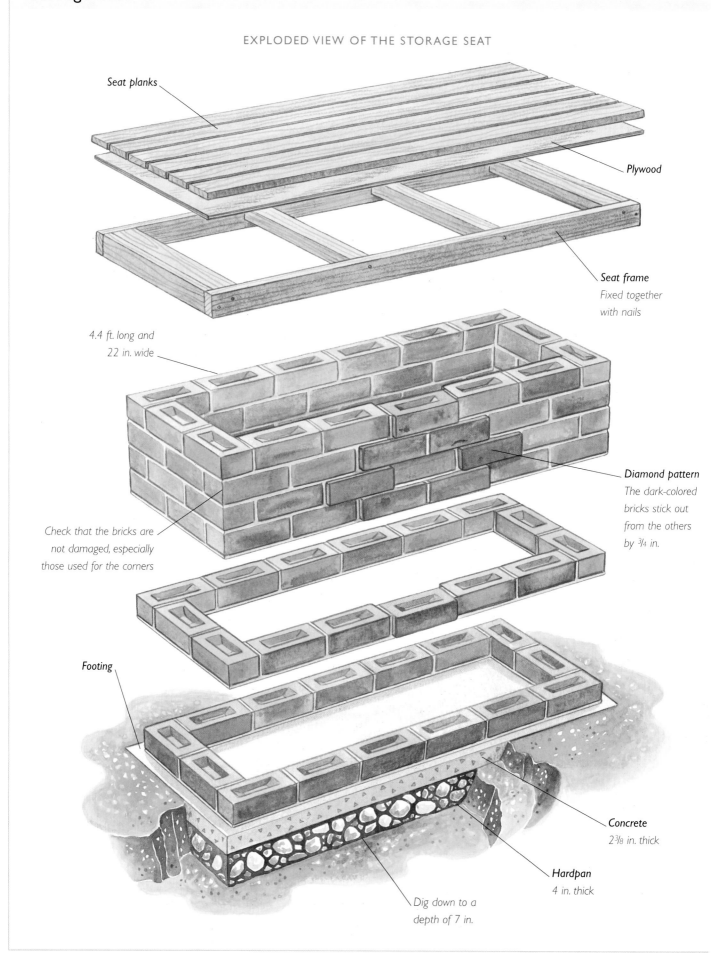

EXPLODED VIEW OF THE STORAGE SEAT

Seat planks

Plywood

Seat frame
Fixed together
with nails

*4.4 ft. long and
22 in. wide*

Diamond pattern
The dark-colored
bricks stick out
from the others
by ³/₄ in.

*Check that the bricks are
not damaged, especially
those used for the corners*

Footing

Concrete
2³/₈ in. thick

Hardpan
4 in. thick

*Dig down to a
depth of 7 in.*

PLAN VIEW SHOWING THE FIRST COURSE OF BRICKS

Concrete footing
4.5 ft. x 25 in.

First course
4.4 ft. x 22 in.

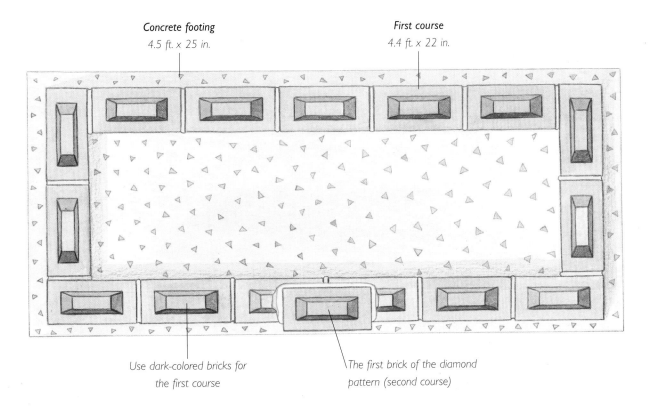

Use dark-colored bricks for the first course

The first brick of the diamond pattern (second course)

CUTAWAY VIEW SHOWING THE WOOD SEAT

Seat planks
6 pieces, 4.5 ft. long, 4 in. wide, and 1 in. thick

Nails
2 in. long

Seat frame is fixed together with 4 in. nails

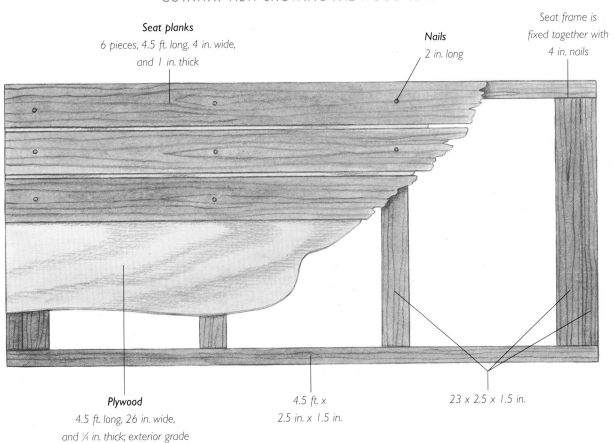

Plywood
4.5 ft. long, 26 in. wide, and ¼ in. thick; exterior grade

4.5 ft. x 2.5 in. x 1.5 in.

23 x 2.5 x 1.5 in.

Step-by-step: **Making the storage seat**

Level
Make sure that the
first course is level

First course
Bed the bricks
on a generous
layer of mortar

1 Chalk out an area, 4.4 ft. long and 22 in. wide, on the footing using the tape measure and a piece of wood for the seat frame. (See page 21 if using an existing footing.) Lay the first course of dark bricks. Make sure that it is level, straight, and the joints are all $1/4$ in. wide.

Helpful hint

If you change the size of the structure, try and keep to using whole bricks. If it is to be built against a wall, build it in the same way— don't be tempted to build just three sides, as it will make the structure very weak.

Second course
Arrange the
second course
so that it is
staggered with
the first

2 Continue laying the bricks, using the light-colored bricks for the rest of the courses and the remaining dark bricks for the diamond pattern. The diamond bricks stick out from the others by $3/4$ in. Stagger the joints in each course.

Hammer
Use the handle
to nudge and
adjust the bricks

Mortar
Before removing excess mortar,
wait until it has partly dried

3 While building the courses, keep checking that the bricks are correctly positioned in a straight line, with equal gaps between them. Take extra care over the bricks used for the pattern, because any mistakes will be obvious. Use the level to check the vertical alignment of the joints within the pattern.

Level
Check the
alignment of
the bricks

Diaper bricks
The dark bricks
forming the
pattern need
to project by
³/4 in.

Pointing
Slide slices of mortar
into the joints

Seat planks
Nail them through the seat
board and into the frame

Mason's trowel
Use this as a
work surface
while you fill
gaps with the
pointing trowel

Seat board
Plywood
sandwiched
between the
planks and
the frame

Nails
Use two short
nails at each
end of the
planks and
one every so
often along
the length

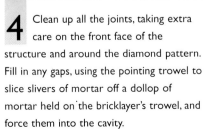

4 Clean up all the joints, taking extra care on the front face of the structure and around the diamond pattern. Fill in any gaps, using the pointing trowel to slice slivers of mortar off a dollop of mortar held on the bricklayer's trowel, and force them into the cavity.

5 Build the seat to fit around the top of the wall (don't forget that the top brick of the diamond pattern sticks out by ³/4 in.). Assemble the seat frame using the long nails, then lay the seat board on top of it and cover it with equally spaced seat planks. Fix with the short nails.

Gateway columns

Get rid of decrepit, leaning wooden fence posts, or ugly concrete blocks, and build a noble gateway in the historic mansion tradition—a bold and dashing piece of garden architecture, which will make a splendid grand entrance to add class to your driveway or front path, or to any part of the garden. The distinctive ball finials magically transform straightforward columns into something special.

TIME

One day to prepare the footing and three days to complete the columns.

SAFETY

If you build columns higher than these, you must also increase their width and depth.

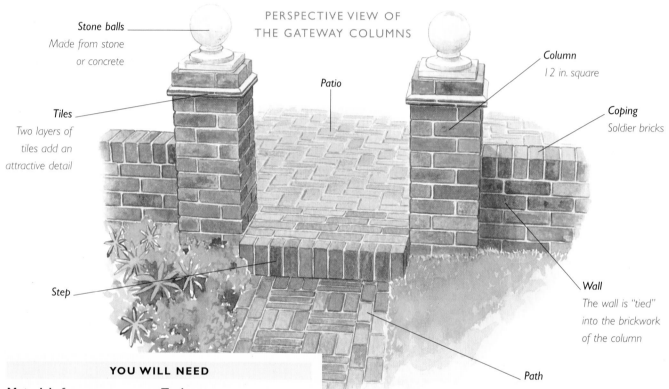

PERSPECTIVE VIEW OF THE GATEWAY COLUMNS

Stone balls
Made from stone or concrete

Tiles
Two layers of tiles add an attractive detail

Step

Patio

Column
12 in. square

Coping
Soldier bricks

Wall
The wall is "tied" into the brickwork of the column

Path

YOU WILL NEED

Materials *for gateway columns 3.75 ft. high and 33 in. apart*
- Bricks: 172
- Tiles: 16 tiles, 8.5 in. long, 6 in. wide, and 0.5 in. thick
- Stone or concrete balls: 2, 11 in. high, with a base 10.5 in. square
- Hardpan: 10.5 cu. feet.
- Concrete: 1 part (265 lb.) portland cement and 4 parts (1060 lb.) ballast
- Mortar: 1 part (44 lb.) portland cement and 4 parts (176 lb.) sand

Tools
- Tape measure, pegs, string, long rule, and a piece of chalk
- Spade and fork
- Wheelbarrow and bucket
- Shovel and mixing board, or cement mixer
- Sledgehammer
- Mason's trowel and pointing trowel
- Brick hammer
- Brick chisel
- Level

MAKING A GRAND ENTRANCE

Historic mansions often have ornate ironwork front gates hung from huge, formal pillars topped by a striking sculpture such as a giant stone eagle. These gateway columns are not so imposing, but they have the same classic pedigree and, in a more restrained way, look grand. We have built them to act as a visual divider between a patio and the rest of the garden, with the columns attached to low brick walls. The columns could also be used either side of a small gate in front of your house, or to span a flight of steps in a terraced garden. They can be used as a feature anywhere in the garden—for example, wherever there is a pathway leading from one distinct area of the garden to another, or where there is a change in levels, you can build columns and divide off the area by adding a brick wall, wooden picket fence, or a beautiful hedge.

Gateway columns

EXPLODED VIEW OF THE GATEWAY COLUMNS

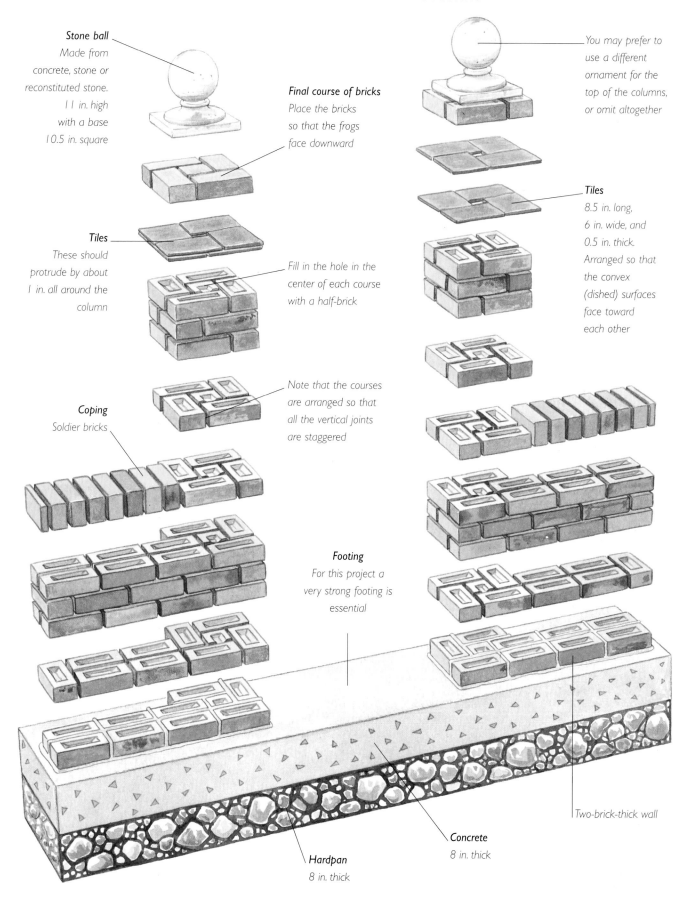

Stone ball
Made from concrete, stone or reconstituted stone. 11 in. high with a base 10.5 in. square

Final course of bricks
Place the bricks so that the frogs face downward

You may prefer to use a different ornament for the top of the columns, or omit altogether

Tiles
These should protrude by about 1 in. all around the column

Fill in the hole in the center of each course with a half-brick

Tiles
8.5 in. long, 6 in. wide, and 0.5 in. thick. Arranged so that the convex (dished) surfaces face toward each other

Coping
Soldier bricks

Note that the courses are arranged so that all the vertical joints are staggered

Footing
For this project a very strong footing is essential

Two-brick-thick wall

Concrete
8 in. thick

Hardpan
8 in. thick

FRONT VIEW OF THE GATEWAY COLUMNS

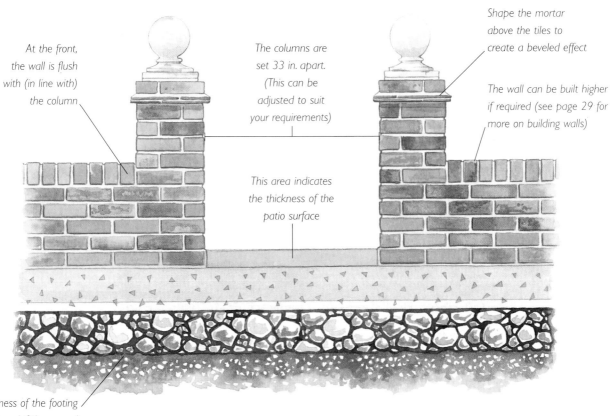

*At the front,
the wall is flush
with (in line with)
the column*

*The columns are
set 33 in. apart.
(This can be
adjusted to suit
your requirements)*

*Shape the mortar
above the tiles to
create a beveled effect*

*The wall can be built higher
if required (see page 29 for
more on building walls)*

*This area indicates
the thickness of the
patio surface*

*The thickness of the footing
can be reduced if the ground
in your garden is unusually
hard*

BACK VIEW OF THE GATEWAY COLUMNS

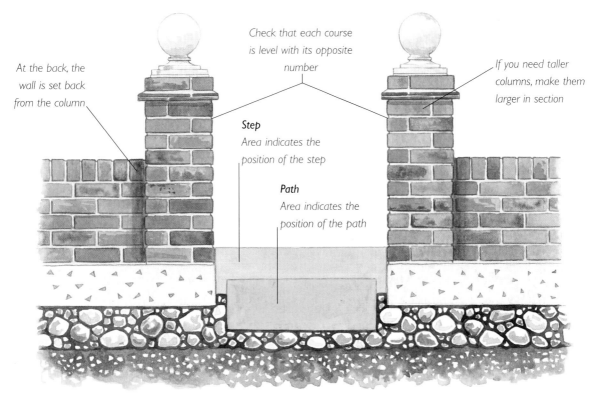

*Check that each course
is level with its opposite
number*

*At the back, the
wall is set back
from the column*

*If you need taller
columns, make them
larger in section*

Step
*Area indicates the
position of the step*

Path
*Area indicates the
position of the path*

Step-by-step: **Making the gateway columns**

Bonds
Study the working drawing carefully

Level
Check that each brick is correctly positioned before placing the next one. Ensure that the corners of the column are true

1 Plan the columns and adjoining walls. If you need steps between the columns, see page 30. Build a footing using at least 8 in. of concrete over 8 in. of compacted hardpan. Mark out the first course and practice laying the bricks without mortar. Lay two courses with mortar, making checks as you go.

Helpful hint

An inadequate footing (too narrow, too thin, or badly made) may cause a pillar to crack or lean. If in doubt, build a bigger footing than you think is needed.

Pointing
Point the joints to a raked finish

Mortar
Ideally, excess mortar should be left alone until it is has dried to a crumbly texture

2 During construction of the columns, clean up the joints between the bricks using the tip of the pointing trowel. Try not to smear mortar on the surface of the bricks (especially wet mortar), and avoid raking out too much mortar from between the bricks.

Soldier brick coping
Lay the bricks on their stretcher face

Pointing the soldier bricks
Point the coping to a smooth finish

Pointing the wall face
Fill any gaps. Rake out the mortar to create a weathered finish

3 Complete laying the courses of the low brick walls, and continue building the columns for another two courses. Lay a coping of soldier bricks, starting at the column end. Use the level and handle of the brick hammer to push the coping into alignment. Clean up the wall joints.

Tiles
Old roof tiles are
perfect for this

4 Continue building the columns, all the time checking that the courses in each column are level with each other and the sides and corners of the columns are vertical. Bed two layers of tiles on mortar in the pattern shown. Note that if the tiles are curved, they should be placed so that the first layer curves upward and the second layer curves downward (and the joints need to be staggered).

Arrangement
Sandwich the
tiles in place so
that the joints
are staggered

Tile overhang
Make sure that
the overhang is
equal all the
way round

5 Build a final course of bricks on top of the tiles, but this time turn the bricks so the frogs are facing downward. Practice positioning the balls on top of the columns, and when you have established the correct position, draw around them with chalk. Spread a layer of mortar inside the marked area and lower the balls into place. Inspect all the brickwork for any gaps that need filling, and clean up the joints as necessary.

Ball finial
Dampen the
base of the
finial prior to
bedding it on
mortar

Frogs
The bricks at the
top of the column
are placed with
the frog facing
downward

Strawberry barrel

How many times have you planted out your strawberries, only to find them eradicated by a slithering army of slugs? This strawberry barrel will help provide a defense by literally lifting your strawberries up to a new level, making access harder for predators. The strawberries are also easier to pick from their elevated position, and make an attractive feature draped over the brickwork.

TIME
One day for the footing and four days to complete the barrel.

SPECIAL TIPS
Don't be tempted to build without a trammel former, because the results will be disappointing.

YOU WILL NEED

Materials *for a strawberry barrel 4 ft. high and 30 in. in diameter*
- Bricks: 117
- Slate: 12 pieces, 9 in. long, 6.5 in. wide, and 0.2 in. thick
- Pebbles: 400, ½–¾ in. in diameter
- Hardpan: 3½ cu. feet
- Concrete: 1 part (66 lb.) portland cement and 4 parts (264 lb.) ballast
- Mortar: 1 part (55 lb.) portland cement and 4 parts (220 lb.) sand
- Wood: 1 piece, 16 in. long, 3 in. wide, and 1 in. thick (trammel former)
- Metal tube: 5 ft. 6 in. long and 1 in. in diameter (trammel former)
- Land drainage pipe: 40 in. long, 4 in. in diameter (for water drainage from the soil)

Tools
- Tape measure, pegs, and string
- Spade
- Wheelbarrow and bucket
- Shovel and mixing board, or cement mixer
- Sledgehammer
- Brick hammer and stonemason's hammer

- Level
- Drill and bit to match diameter of the metal tube
- Mole grips
- Brick chisel
- Mason's trowel and pointing trowel
- Rubber mallet
- Tile cutter

A STRAWBERRY PASSION

This sculptural planter is specifically designed for growing strawberries and presenting them in a decorative way. It is probably best to build it in a sunny spot to one side of the garden, or as the centerpiece of a vegetable patch or decorative cottage garden. If you intend to use the structure to plant flowers instead, you may want to incorporate more pockets, and reserve the shady side for plants that don't need as much sun.

The height of the barrel can be reduced if required. The whole barrel is built using half-bricks, so choose bricks that break in half easily. The structure looks complicated, but it is in fact simple to build as the trammel former (see page 27) seems to do all the work for you. Make the strawberry barrel something to be proud of—take care over the joints and don't skimp on the decorative pebbles pressed into the mortar.

Trammel former
Used during construction

FRONT VIEW SHOWING THE FOOTING AND TRAMMEL FORMER

Half-bricks

Planting pocket
One brick is left out and the gap is bridged using a piece of slate

Concrete
4 in. thick

Metal tube
Set upright in concrete. Forms a pivot for the trammel former

Hardpan
6 in. thick

Strawberry barrel

EXPLODED VIEW OF THE STRAWBERRY BARREL

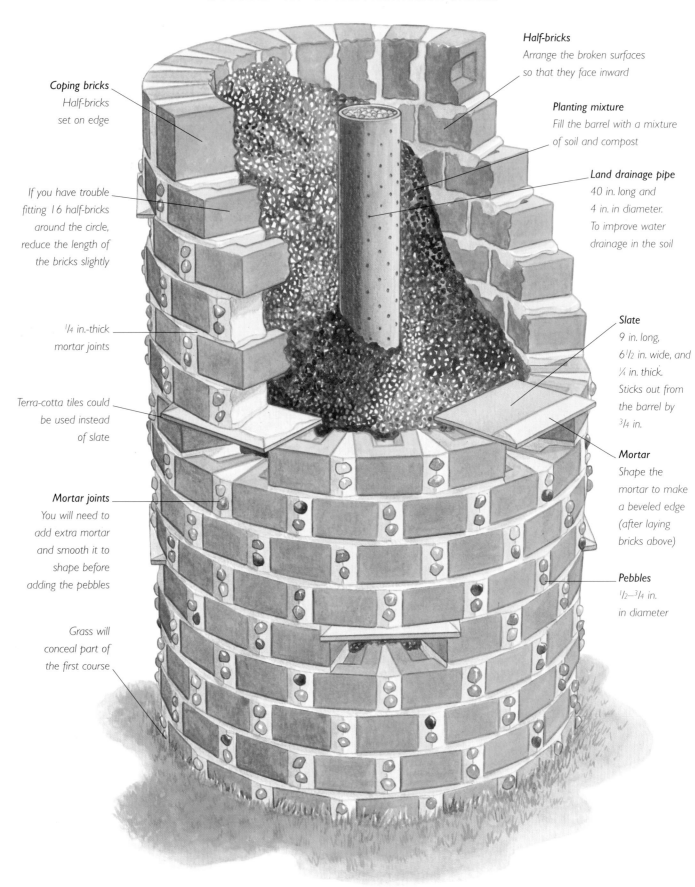

Coping bricks
Half-bricks
set on edge

If you have trouble
fitting 16 half-bricks
around the circle,
reduce the length of
the bricks slightly

1/4 in.-thick
mortar joints

Terra-cotta tiles could
be used instead
of slate

Mortar joints
You will need to
add extra mortar
and smooth it to
shape before
adding the pebbles

Grass will
conceal part of
the first course

Half-bricks
Arrange the broken surfaces
so that they face inward

Planting mixture
Fill the barrel with a mixture
of soil and compost

Land drainage pipe
40 in. long and
4 in. in diameter.
To improve water
drainage in the soil

Slate
9 in. long,
6 1/2 in. wide, and
1/4 in. thick.
Sticks out from
the barrel by
3/4 in.

Mortar
Shape the
mortar to make
a beveled edge
(after laying
bricks above)

Pebbles
1/2—3/4 in.
in diameter

PLAN VIEW SHOWING THE TRAMMEL AND A COMPLETE COURSE OF BRICKS

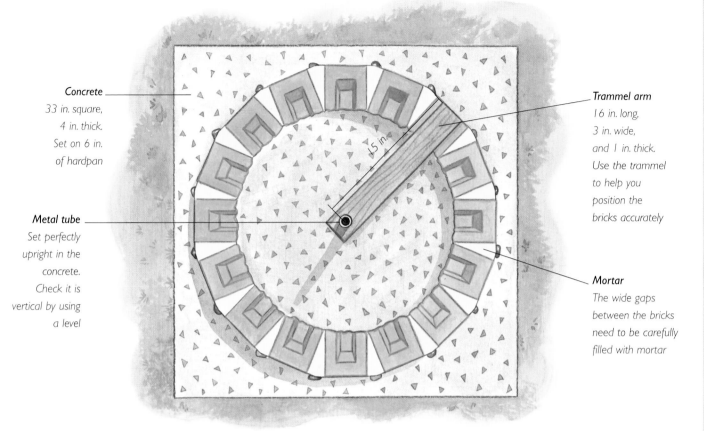

Concrete
33 in. square,
4 in. thick.
Set on 6 in.
of hardpan

Metal tube
Set perfectly
upright in the
concrete.
Check it is
vertical by using
a level

15 in.

Trammel arm
16 in. long,
3 in. wide,
and 1 in. thick.
Use the trammel
to help you
position the
bricks accurately

Mortar
The wide gaps
between the bricks
need to be carefully
filled with mortar

PLAN VIEW SHOWING THE LAYOUT OF THE SLATES OVER THE PLANTING POCKETS

After each course
of bricks, raise the
trammel former by
2$\frac{1}{2}$ in. (the
thickness of a brick
plus $\frac{1}{4}$ in. of
mortar) and
support it at the
center by clamping
a pair of mole grips
underneath it

Position the slate
so that it sticks out
from the side of
the barrel by
$\frac{3}{4}$ in. Use the
trammel former
as a guide

The slate should
be placed centrally
over the pocket of
space beneath

Step-by-step: **Making the strawberry barrel**

Mole grips
Slide up the tube until the trammel arm is at the correct height

Positioning
Set each brick square with the end of the trammel former

Trammel former arm
Establishes the correct position for the bricks

Drainage
The wood ensures an open joint for drainage

Leveling
Tap the trammel former until the brick is level

1 Build a level footing. While the concrete is still wet, knock the metal tube into the center of the footing. Check that it is vertical using the level. When the concrete is dry, make a trammel former (see page 27). This pivots on the metal tube. Use mole grips to hold the trammel arm up. Practice laying the first course of half-bricks and check that you can fit sixteen around the circle.

2 Mix up the mortar and start laying the first course of bricks, bedding them level on $1/4$ in.-thick mortar and using the trammel former as a positional guide. Leave a scrap of wood between two of the bricks to create a water drainage hole (pull out on completion). Use the rubber mallet, on top of the end of the trammel arm, to knock the bricks down. Check that the course is level by using the level.

3 Continue building further courses. After each course is complete, create angled mortar joints between the bricks and push two small pebbles into each one. This takes a bit of practice to get right, so be prepared to scrape out the first few joints and start over again.

Mortar
Angle a wedge of mortar between the bricks

Decoration
Push the pebbles into the soft mortar

Mole grips
Slide the grips up until level with the slate

Slate
Push the slate outward so that it overhangs by about 3/4 in.

4 Continue building upward until you get to the fifth course. On this course, leave out four bricks to create each planting pocket. Cut pieces of slate or imitation slate and use these to bridge the gaps, the slate sticking out from the barrel by 3/4 in. After laying the next course, spread mortar over the part of the slate that sticks out.

Helpful hint

Take care when fitting the pieces of slate—place them so that sharp edges face inward, or smooth the edges and corners with a circular saw with masonry blade. Clay tiles could be used instead of slate.

Soldier course
Arrange the half-bricks on their stretcher face for a decorative finish

5 After each course that includes planting pockets, lay three complete courses of bricks before the next course of planting pockets. After completing three courses with planting pockets, creating a total of twelve pockets, build a final course of bricks on top, followed by a soldier course. Fill all the joints with mortar, finish them with the pointing trowel, and stud with pebbles (not on the soldier course). After a few days, remove the metal tube by repeatedly bending it until it snaps off. Put a layer of crocks in the bottom of the barrel for drainage, followed by the drainage pipe. Hold it upright as you fill the strawberry barrel with soil. Plant the pockets with strawberry plants.

Semicircular steps

You might think that a doorstep is just a block of brickwork that enables you to move easily from one level to another, but that is only part of its function. Front doorsteps are traditionally built to make a grand, welcoming feature. The curved form of these steps makes attractive terracing, where there is plenty of space to set out a display of pot plants to make the entrance to the house look even more appealing.

TIME
Four days to build (five if you need a footing).

SAFETY
Ensure that the surface of the steps is smooth, with no slightly raised areas that might cause people to trip. The steps must be correctly spaced for your site. (See page 30.)

YOU WILL NEED

Materials *for semicircular steps about 7 ft. long, 3.5 ft. wide, and 12 in. high*
- Bricks: 168
- Hardpan: 9 cu. feet
- Concrete: 1 part (220 lb.) portland cement; 4 parts (880 lb.) ballast
- Mortar: 1 part (44 lb.) portland cement and 4 parts (176 lb.) sand
- Wood: 1 piece, 10 ft. long, 1.5 in. wide, and 1 in. thick (long rule and trammel former); 1 piece, 12 in. long and 3 in. square, and 1 piece, 18 in. long, 4 in. wide, and 2 in. thick (tamping beams)
- Masonry nails: 2 x 6 in. (trammel pivot and guide)

Tools
- Tape measure and chalk
- Spade
- Wheelbarrow and bucket
- Shovel and mixing board, or cement mixer
- Sledgehammer
- Claw hammer
- Level
- Mason's trowel and pointing trowel
- Brick hammer, brick chisel

A STEP UP FROM THE REST

First impressions count—or at least that is what people say when they meet somebody new—and the same applies to the entrance to your house. These decorative steps, with an interesting patterned surface, will definitely make a good impression, and their generous size provides a comfortable standing area.

When planning steps, one of the most important factors is the height of each step (the riser measurement). Steps should be no greater than 9 in. high, and no less than 2½ in. high (a good average would be 6 in.).

You may need to adjust the design to suit your site (see page 30 about planning steps). If you have a paved surface surrounding the area of the steps, consider how you will repair it after the job is finished.

Mark out and build a concrete footing that slopes away from the house slightly (about 1 in. per 6½ ft.): remove existing paving and dig a footing 8 in. deep, fill it with compacted hardpan 4 in. thick, and top with 4 in. of concrete.

CROSS-SECTION DETAIL OF THE SEMICIRCULAR STEPS

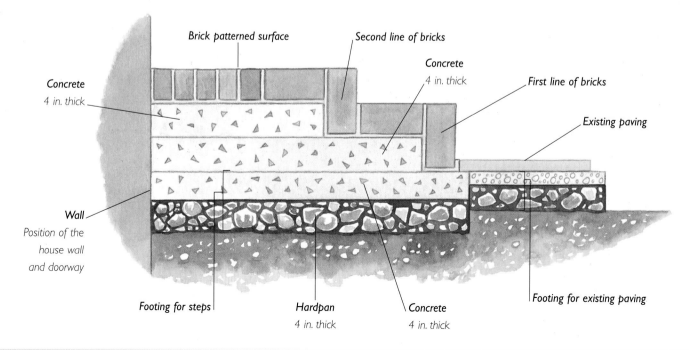

Brick patterned surface

Second line of bricks

Concrete
4 in. thick

First line of bricks

Concrete
4 in. thick

Existing paving

Wall
Position of the house wall and doorway

Footing for steps

Hardpan
4 in. thick

Concrete
4 in. thick

Footing for existing paving

Semicircular steps

PLAN VIEW OF THE SEMICIRCULAR STEPS

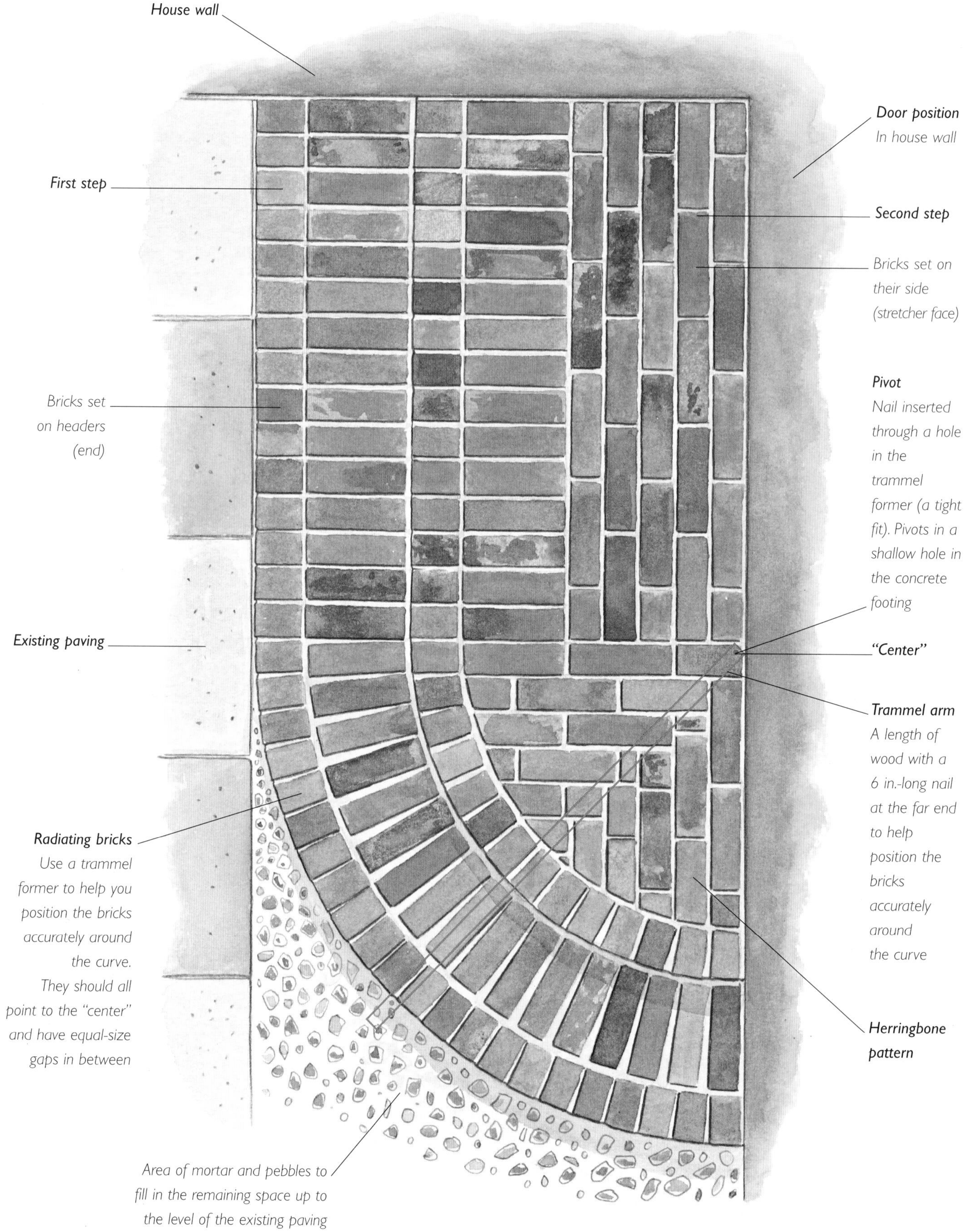

House wall

Door position
In house wall

First step

Second step

Bricks set on
their side
(stretcher face)

Bricks set
on headers
(end)

Pivot
*Nail inserted
through a hole
in the
trammel
former (a tight
fit). Pivots in a
shallow hole in
the concrete
footing*

Existing paving

"Center"

Trammel arm
*A length of
wood with a
6 in.-long nail
at the far end
to help
position the
bricks
accurately
around
the curve*

Radiating bricks
*Use a trammel
former to help you
position the bricks
accurately around
the curve.
They should all
point to the "center"
and have equal-size
gaps in between*

Herringbone
pattern

*Area of mortar and pebbles to
fill in the remaining space up to
the level of the existing paving*

EXPLODED VIEW OF THE SEMICIRCULAR STEPS

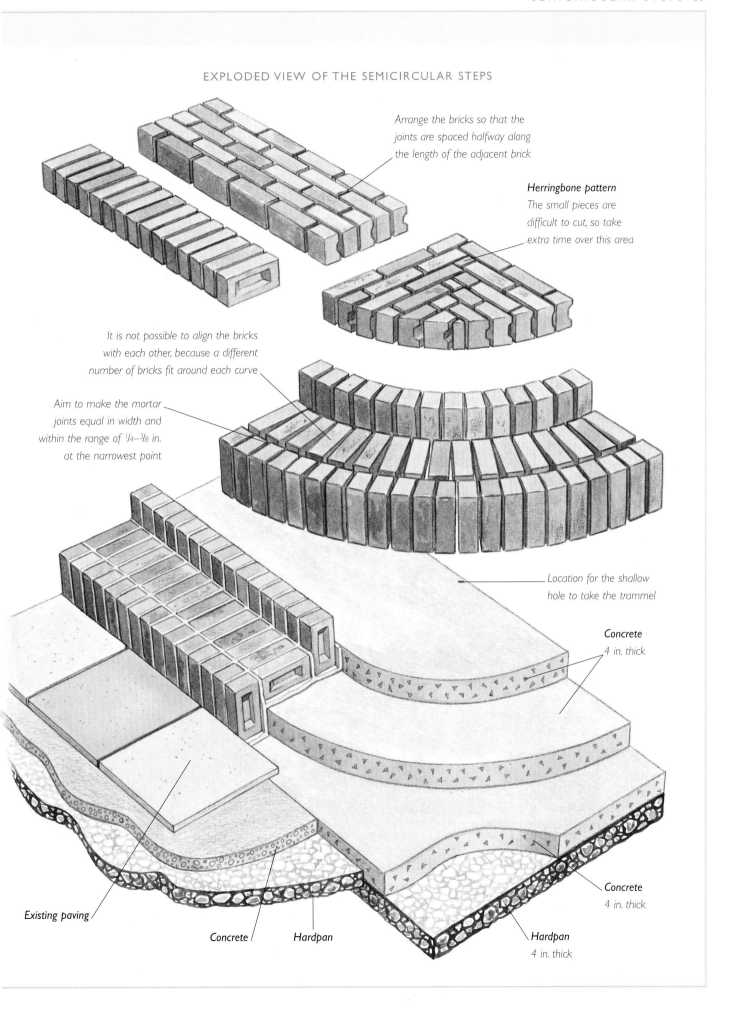

Arrange the bricks so that the joints are spaced halfway along the length of the adjacent brick

Herringbone pattern
The small pieces are difficult to cut, so take extra time over this area

It is not possible to align the bricks with each other, because a different number of bricks fit around each curve

Aim to make the mortar joints equal in width and within the range of $^1/_4$–$^3/_8$ in. at the narrowest point

Location for the shallow hole to take the trammel

Concrete
4 in. thick

Concrete
4 in. thick

Existing paving

Concrete

Hardpan

Hardpan
4 in. thick

Step-by-step: **Making the semicircular steps**

Soldier bricks
Set the bricks upright
on their header face

Concrete
Depth must allow for (on top) a
brick on its side plus $^1/_4$ in.

Trammel
former
Has a hanging
nail to facilitate
the aligning of
the bricks

Tamping
Use waste
wood to
tamp the
concrete level

Outer edge of
bottom step
Area within is
filled with
concrete

1 Build the outer edge of the bottom step from soldier bricks set on end, using the trammel former (see page 27) and level to guide you. Butter the frog face with mortar, and lay each brick on $^1/_4$ in. of mortar. The straight bricks have $^1/_4$ in. of mortar between them, and the bricks following the curve have a minimum of $^1/_4$ in. of mortar between them.

2 Fill the area within the outer edge with concrete to a level depth that leaves room for a layer of bricks on their stretcher face plus $^1/_4$ in. of mortar. Use the shorter tamping beam to spread the concrete and check that it is level. If in doubt, it is better to err on the side of having the concrete a bit lower (and later use extra mortar to build up the bricks to the correct level). Leave the concrete to dry.

Alignment
The bricks
must point
towards the
"center" of
the trammel

Trammel
former
Check the
alignment of
every brick

Step level
Ensure that the
soldier bricks
are upright

3 Spread a bed of mortar over the concrete and use the trammel former and level to help you lay the curve of bricks. The gaps between the bricks won't line up with the outer edge, but try to maintain equal-thickness gaps, and make sure all the bricks around the curve point to the "center" (see working drawing).

4 Build the outer edge of the top step on the same slab of concrete and again use the trammel to guide you around the curve. Check that the tops of the bricks are level with the bottom of the doorway. Let the mortar between the bricks dry before proceeding to the next stage.

Concrete
Depth must allow for (on top) a
brick on its side plus ¹/₄ in.

Tamping
Tamp the
concrete level

Brick level
Keep checking
that the bricks
remain true

5 Fill the area inside the outer edge of the top step with concrete as described in step 2. Tamp with the longer tamping beam. There should be enough space to lay the final bricks on a ¹/₄ in.-thick bed of mortar.

Pattern
This area of
pattern is what
people will notice
first when they
approach your
door. If you are
worried about
fitting the bricks
into the space, or
think you might
make a mistake,
practice setting
out the bricks in
the design before
spreading mortar

6 When the concrete has set, fill in the top step with bricks in the two patterns illustrated. Lay the straight line of staggered bricks first, then finish with the 90° pattern that fills the curved area. Cut the bricks to shape using the brick hammer and brick chisel. Fill the joints with a dryish mixture of mortar and tidy them up with the pointing trowel.

Helpful hint

When you are leveling the bricks, try to make them end up sloping away from the house slightly.

Inspirations: Brick steps

Nothing beats bricks for versatility when it comes to building steps. They can be set with the frog face or the bottom face uppermost, on their end (header), or on their side (stretcher) in order to create different effects and levels. They can be cut or angled, and laid in a variety of patterns on the treads. Bricks harmonize with stone and tiles—designs for steps can successfully comprise a mixture of materials. Best of all, bricks are wonderfully easy to handle and make step-building a pleasure.

FAR RIGHT This solidly well-built flight of steps connects a path to a beautiful brick yard. The design appears effortless, but in fact great care has gone into planning the overall brickwork scheme and incorporating steps that are subtly curved.

ABOVE A decorative, low-rise set of two steps in a country garden. Notice how the shape and sweeping arrangement of the steps leads the eye across the patio to the other steps and the lawn beyond. The framed herringbone pattern and recessed detailing must have been a challenge to build.

RIGHT This step started life as a small step (the two-brick-wide section near the door). When the owner wanted the step made deeper, the bricklayer simply added a band of clay roof tiles set on edge plus another row of bricks on edge. The tiles add decorative interest to what would otherwise be a plain step.

Tudor arch wall niche

A niche in a wall always invites questions. What is it for? Is it a shrine? Is it a blocked-up window? When was it built? So if you want to create a bit of intrigue in your garden, this project is ideal. In Tudor times, bricks first came to be used in a decorative way, and this niche has been inspired by Tudor arches. It is an exciting but complex project to build—an enjoyably skill-testing challenge.

TIME

Six days (do not lay more than four courses in one day).

SAFETY

See page 29 for information on walls and requirements for piers and buttresses.

YOU WILL NEED

Materials *for Tudor arch wall niche 5.2 ft. high and 4.7 ft. wide*
- Bricks: 276
- Stone slab: 1 piece, 22 in. long, 10 in. wide, and 1.5 in. thick (sill)
- Hardpan: 3.5 cu. feet.
- Sand: 1 shovelful
- Concrete: 1 part (66 lb.) portland cement and 4 parts (264 lb.) ballast
- Mortar: 1 part (66 lb.) portland cement and 4 parts (264 lb.) sand
- Wood: 10 pieces, 3.5 in. long, 1 in. wide, and 1 in. thick (sticks for center of former); 1 piece, 28 in. long, 1.5 in. wide, and 1 in. thick (trammel former)
- Plywood: 2 pieces, 22 in. long, 5 in. wide, and ¼ in. thick (former)
- Nails: 20 x 1.5 in.

Tools
- Tape measure, pegs, string, long rule, and piece of chalk
- Spade
- Wheelbarrow and bucket
- Shovel and mixing board, or cement mixer
- Sledgehammer
- Mason's trowel and pointing trowel
- Brick hammer and stonemason's hammer
- Brick chisel
- Rubber mallet
- Level
- Handsaw
- Jigsaw
- Claw hammer

A FINE DISPLAY

The recess or niche is decorative in itself, but it also acts like a picture frame for anything you want to display in it. We have put a statuette in this one, but yours could display a mosaic picture, salvaged cartwheel, or curious antique. Other ideas include a wall mask fixed in the recess, spouting water into a stone trough, or the whole arch can be built deeper and bigger and the sill made into a narrow seat for perching on—a kind of brick arbor.

This project is a little more challenging than the others, because you need to keep all the vertical joints in the coursework aligned. This ensures that the sides of the archway are well presented. However, the finished results are well worth the effort.

FRONT VIEW OF THE TUDOR ARCH WALL NICHE

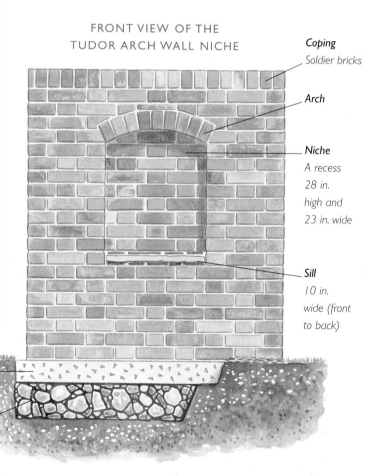

Coping
Soldier bricks

Arch

Niche
A recess 28 in. high and 23 in. wide

Sill
10 in. wide (front to back)

Concrete
5 in. thick

Hardpan
8 in. thick

Tudor arch wall niche

FRONT VIEW OF THE ARCH FORMER (ONE SIDE REMOVED)

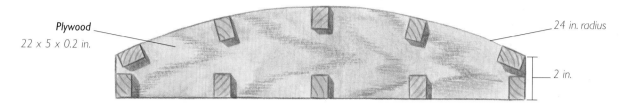

Plywood
22 x 5 x 0.2 in.

24 in. radius

2 in.

EXPLODED VIEW OF THE ARCH FORMER

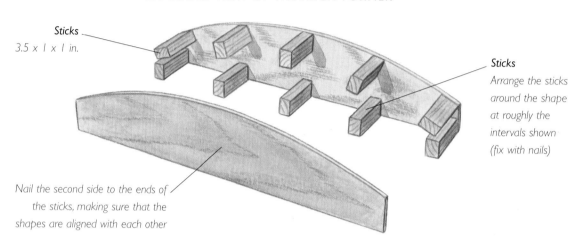

Sticks
3.5 x 1 x 1 in.

Sticks
Arrange the sticks
around the shape
at roughly the
intervals shown
(fix with nails)

Nail the second side to the ends of
the sticks, making sure that the
shapes are aligned with each other

FRONT VIEW SHOWING HOW TO SUPPORT THE FORMER

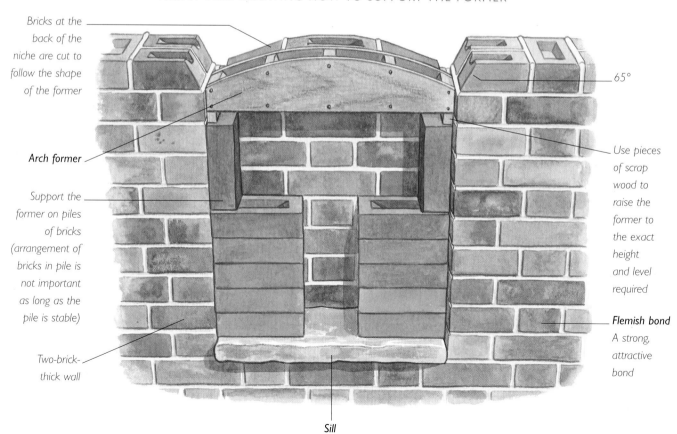

Bricks at the
back of the
niche are cut to
follow the shape
of the former

Arch former

Support the
former on piles
of bricks
(arrangement of
bricks in pile is
not important
as long as the
pile is stable)

Two-brick-
thick wall

65°

Use pieces
of scrap
wood to
raise the
former to
the exact
height
and level
required

Flemish bond
A strong,
attractive
bond

Sill
Stone slab, 22 x 10 x 1.5 in.

EXPLODED VIEW OF THE TUDOR ARCH WALL NICHE

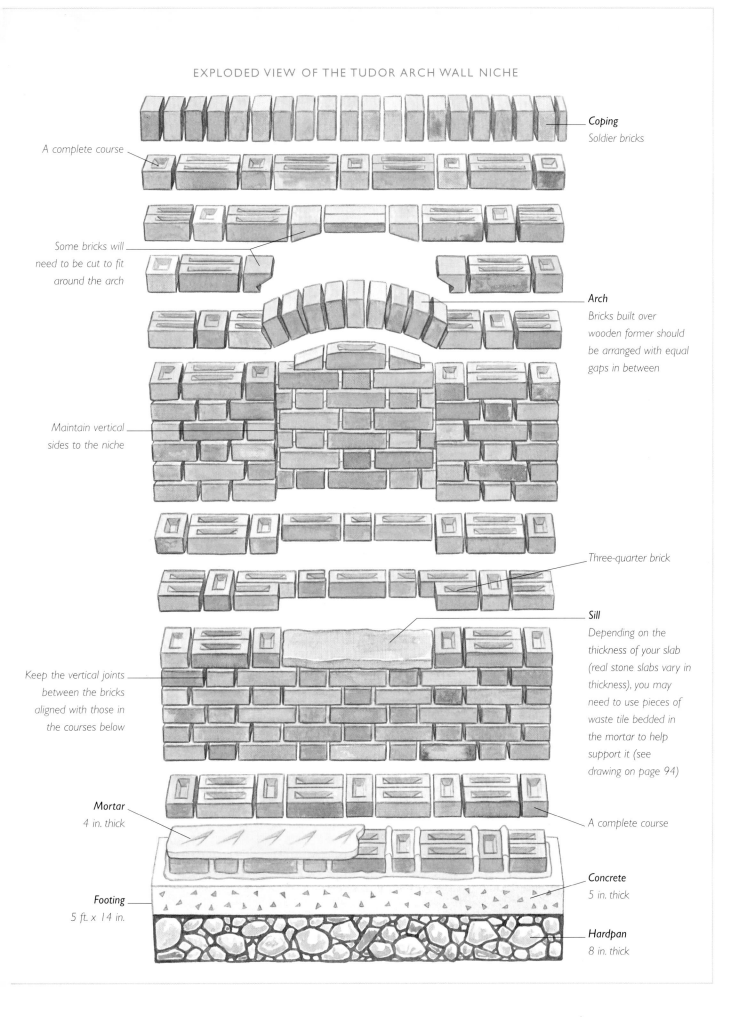

A complete course

Coping
Soldier bricks

Some bricks will need to be cut to fit around the arch

Arch
Bricks built over wooden former should be arranged with equal gaps in between

Maintain vertical sides to the niche

Three-quarter brick

Sill
Depending on the thickness of your slab (real stone slabs vary in thickness), you may need to use pieces of waste tile bedded in the mortar to help support it (see drawing on page 94)

Keep the vertical joints between the bricks aligned with those in the courses below

Mortar
4 in. thick

A complete course

Concrete
5 in. thick

Footing
5 ft. x 14 in.

Hardpan
8 in. thick

Step-by-step: **Making the Tudor arch wall niche**

Wall
*Build a base wall to
the required sill height*

1 Build a footing 5 ft. long and 14 in. wide, consisting of a 8 in.-thick layer of hardpan topped with a 5 in.-thick layer of concrete. When the concrete is dry, lay the first course of bricks. Note that this wall is two bricks thick, and is built using Flemish bond. Continue building the wall until you have completed seven courses. Use a long rule, level, and rubber mallet to help double-check the level and straightness of the wall. Scrape out and clean the joints before the mortar dries.

Bond
*Flemish bond
results in an
extremely
strong bond*

2 On the eighth course, leave a central space for the slab. Check that your stone sill is the correct size by placing it on the wall. The ends should align with joints between the bricks of the sixth course (if not, cut to size). Position the slab on a generous bed of mortar and coat it with sand to protect the surface during the rest of the building operation. The slab protrudes from the wall by 1 ½ in.

Leveling
*Use mortar, and
if necessary
scraps of slate,
to ensure the
sill is level*

Sill
*Ease the sill
outward so that
it protrudes by
1 ½ in.*

Single-thickness wall
Use half-bricks to create the illusion of a Flemish bond

Former
The former can be rough and ready, as long as it does the job

Corners
Make sure that the corners are vertically true

Alignment
The curved pieces must be aligned with each other

Plywood
Draw the shape of the former by using a grid to plot the curve, or use a trammel to draw an arc with a radius of 24 in.

3 Continue building upward for a further eight courses, reducing the wall to a single thickness at the back of the slab, creating a niche. Study the working drawings to see how the bricks are placed for the best effect.

4 Build a wooden former to support the arch during construction. (See page 27 for information about trammel formers.) Cut out the pieces with the jigsaw and join together—place one of the sticks underneath and hammer through the plywood into the stick. Nail on the rest of the sticks in the same way, then put the other sheet of plywood on top, and nail through into the sticks.

Practice
t is a good idea to practice arranging bricks on top of the former. Once you have a feel for the gaps, it is necessary to leave between each brick, it is more likely that you will arrange them correctly when building with mortar. Angle them so they are all aimed at a central point on the sill.

5 Support the former on piles of bricks. Continue building the single-brick-thick wall behind it, cutting bricks to follow the shape of the curve. Complete the course either side of the arch using angled bricks to support it (see diagram). Lay the top of the arch over the former, maintaining equal gaps between the bricks. Build two courses above the arch, cutting bricks as necessary. Finish with a soldier brick coping.

Helpful hint

You risk damaging the formwork if you knock the bricks too hard. It is better to take your time applying the correct amount of mortar to each brick.

Classic round pond

There is something complete and rather satisfying about a circular pool of water. This sunken pond is interesting to build and makes a beautiful feature that will suit most styles of garden. We have built it to fit snugly into a patio, where it can be surrounded by an ever-changing display of container plants to give the pond a distinct seasonal character.

TIME
Two days to dig the hole and four to five days to complete the brickwork.

SPECIAL TIPS
If you have young children, it is better not to have a pond in your garden.

YOU WILL NEED

Materials *for a pond 6.6 ft. in diameter and 3 ft. deep*
- Bricks: 220 (walls) and 47 (top edge)
- Concrete: 1 part (160 lb.) portland cement and 4 parts (635 lb.) ballast
- Mortar: 1 part (110 lb.) portland cement and 3 parts (330 lb.) sand
- Soft sand: 1.1 tons
- Wood:
  1 piece, 6 ft. long, 4 in. wide, and 2 in. thick, and 2 pieces, 4 ft. long, 4 in. wide, and 1 in. thick (tamping beam with handles);
  1 piece, 8 in. long, 3 in. wide, and 3 in. thick (trammel former support block);
  1 piece, 4 ft. long, 2.5 in. wide, and 1 in. thick (trammel arm);
  and 1 piece, 6 ft. long, 4 in. wide, and 1 in. thick (beam to check level)
- Plywood: 1 piece, 20 in. square and ¼ in. thick (trammel base), and 1 piece, 18 in. long, 12 in. wide, and ¼ in. thick (U-shaped trammel piece)
- Synthetic padding: 398 sq. feet
- Pond-grade Butyl rubber liner: 1 piece, 14 ft. square
- Nails: 5 x 2.5 in.

Tools
- Tape measure, pegs, string, marking chalk, or aerosol marker
- Spade and fork
- Wheelbarrow and bucket
- Scissors
- Handsaw
- Claw hammer
- Shovel and mixing board, or cement mixer
- Jigsaw
- Portable workbench
- Mason's trowel and pointing trowel
- Brick hammer
- Level
- Sledgehammer

LAYOUT OF THE FIRST COURSE OF BRICKS

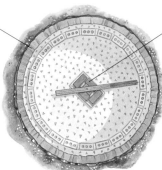

Pond lining
A combination of butyl rubber and synthetic padding runs under the concrete footing and up behind the wall

Trammel former
Use a length of wood pivoted at the center of the pond to indicate the correct positioning of the wall bricks (see also page 27)

LAYOUT OF THE TOP EDGE BRICKS

Edge bricks
These are laid with equal-size gaps in between

Portable workbench
Supports trammel

Trammel former
The same setup as above, but extended using a piece of plywood with the shape of a brick cut out of it

CIRCLE POWER

This round, sunken brick pond is a classic. A pond often becomes the focal point of a garden or yard, and can be treated in different ways—you can populate it with fish, plant a glorious display of water-lilies, or install a water feature.

There are important safety factors to take into account if you are considering building a pond. If you have young children, it is safer not to have a pond. (To protect visiting children, make a slatted wooden lid to cover the pond for short periods.)

Avoid excavating areas where there is a likelihood of uncovering pipes and drains—as a general rule, always dig carefully and if you encounter any, seek expert advice. (See also page 38.) If you want to install a fountain, incorporate armored plastic pipe (2 in. in diameter) to protect the pump cable, which will run across the bottom of the pond (on top of the liner), through a hole in the wall, up between the wall and the liner, over the edge of the liner, and then be buried under paving slabs.

Classic round pond

CUTAWAY CROSS-SECTION VIEW OF THE CLASSIC ROUND POND

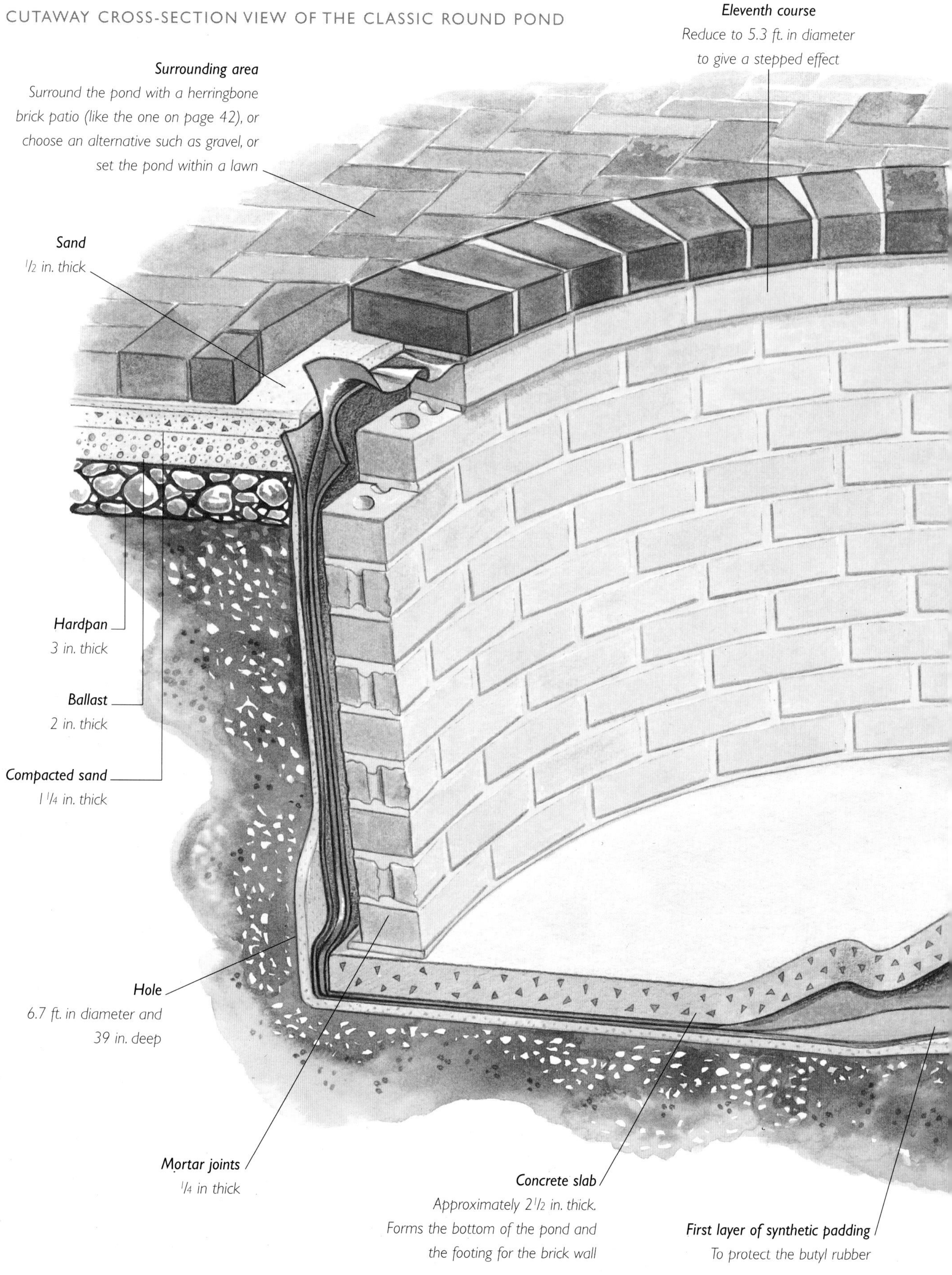

Surrounding area
*Surround the pond with a herringbone
brick patio (like the one on page 42), or
choose an alternative such as gravel, or
set the pond within a lawn*

Sand
$1/2$ in. thick

Eleventh course
*Reduce to 5.3 ft. in diameter
to give a stepped effect*

Hardpan
3 in. thick

Ballast
2 in. thick

Compacted sand
$1 1/4$ in. thick

Hole
*6.7 ft. in diameter and
39 in. deep*

Mortar joints
$1/4$ in thick

Concrete slab
*Approximately $2 1/2$ in. thick.
Forms the bottom of the pond and
the footing for the brick wall*

First layer of synthetic padding
To protect the butyl rubber

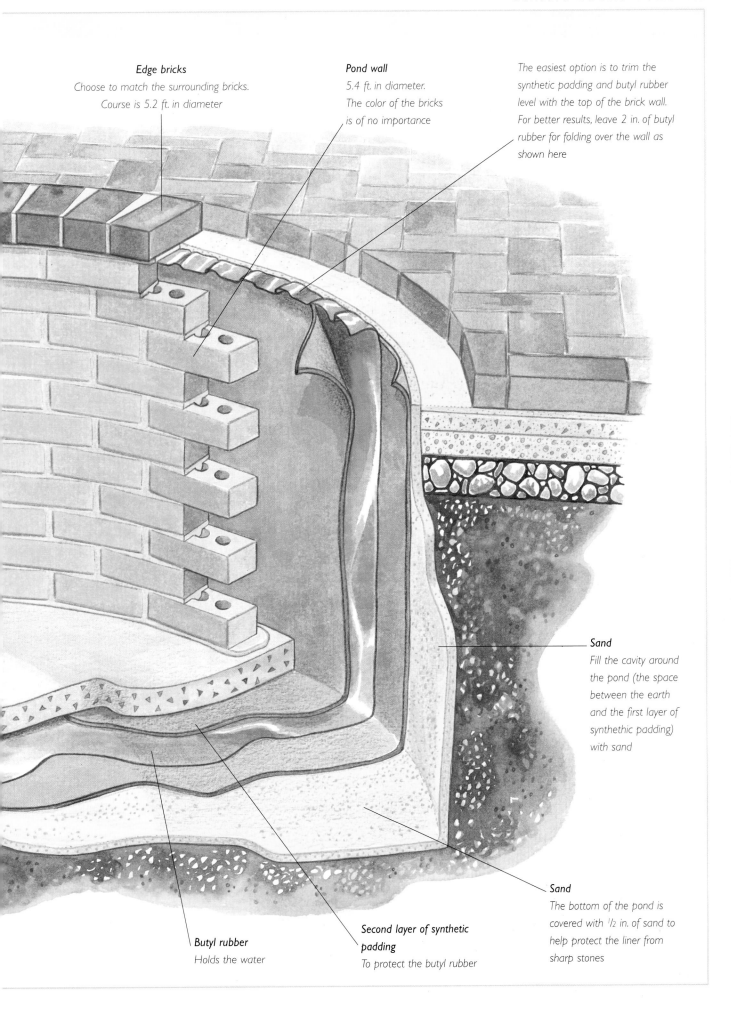

Edge bricks
Choose to match the surrounding bricks.
Course is 5.2 ft. in diameter

Pond wall
5.4 ft. in diameter.
The color of the bricks
is of no importance

The easiest option is to trim the
synthetic padding and butyl rubber
level with the top of the brick wall.
For better results, leave 2 in. of butyl
rubber for folding over the wall as
shown here

Sand
Fill the cavity around
the pond (the space
between the earth
and the first layer of
synthethic padding)
with sand

Sand
The bottom of the pond is
covered with $1/2$ in. of sand to
help protect the liner from
sharp stones

Butyl rubber
Holds the water

**Second layer of synthetic
padding**
To protect the butyl rubber

Step-by-step: **Making the classic round pond**

Digging
Work slowly, so the sides
of the hole don't collapse

Top
Use bricks to hold the
top of the padding

Hole shape
If the earth at
the sides
crumbles, make
the hole wider
at the top

Sides
Be generous
and leave a
big overlap

Bottom
Remove sharp
stones before
laying the
synthetic
padding

1 Mark out a circle 6.7 ft. in diameter
(and a patio area if required), and dig
out the earth to a depth of 39 in. The soil
may crumble a little at the edges, but this
is not a problem as long as the hole is at
least 6.7 ft. in diameter at the bottom. If
the ground is hard and rocky, break it up
with a pick or mattock.

2 Remove sharp stones from the hole
and line it with sand followed by
synthetic padding. Cover the bottom first
and then drape it up the sides, with evenly
distributed folds and overlaps of 4 in. or
more at the joins. Make sure that it
overlaps the top of the hole by at least
12 in. Weigh down the edges with bricks.

Butyl rubber
Use bricks to hold the
top edge in place

Synthetic padding
Cover the butyl rubber
with padding as in step 2

Sides
Try to distribute
the folds
equally around
the sides

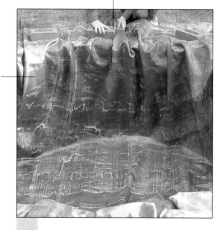

Tamping
Tamp the
concrete level
right up to
the sides of
the hole

Concrete
Lay a 2½ in.-
thick slab on
top of the
synthetic
padding

3 Cover the synthetic padding with a
single sheet of butyl rubber. (Don't
put water in the hole to help spread it.)
Keep rearranging it so that it takes up the
shape of the pond and the folds are evenly
distributed. It should overlap the edge of
the pond by at least 12 in.; weigh down the
top edge with bricks.

4 Spread a second layer of synthetic
padding over the butyl rubber, then
overlap the edges and weigh it down. Ask a
friend to help you lay a slab of 2½ in.-thick
concrete in the bottom of the pond,
smoothing it out with a tamping beam (fix
handles to the beam with nails) operated
from ground level. Leave the concrete to
dry for two days.

Horizontal level

Check the level of every course of bricks

Vertical level

Use the level to ensure that the walls are vertical and true

5 Build a round brick wall, ten bricks high, on top of the concrete (diameter is approx. 5.4 ft). You may prefer to use a trammel former to establish the circle (see pages 27 and 100). Leave 1/4 in.-thick mortar joints, then scrape away excess mortar and clean the joints before the mortar dries. Check vertical and horizontal levels during construction. Add an eleventh course, overlapping the previous one by about 1/2 in., to give a decorative stepped edge to the pond (diameter is 5.3 ft.).

Trammel former

Use to ensure the edge forms a true circle

Patio

If you are going to surround the pond with a patio, dig out the earth around the pond. Spread 2 in. of hardpan, 1 1/4 in. of compacted ballast, and 1/2 in. of uncompacted sharp sand over the area

6 Fold the pond lining (padding and butyl rubber) over the wall and into the pond. Fill the cavity between the wall and the earth with sand. Trim the lining level with the bricks. Make a trammel former (or if you used one in step 5, extend it) that indicates a circle 5.2 ft. in diameter, and lay the twelfth course of bricks around the edge of the pond. The former consists of a plywood base, placed on a workbench. The base holds the trammel support block, surrounded by bricks to weigh down the base. The trammel arm pivots on a nail in the support block. A U-shaped trammel piece is fixed to the arm to indicate the position of the edge bricks, which are laid to meet the end of the former at 90°. Finish work on the surrounding area.

Inspirations: Decorative brickwork

Bricks are inherently decorative in their own right, with a color range that ascends

from slate blue and black to red, encompassing a rainbow of oranges, yellows, and

umbers in between. The other beauty of bricks is that they can be laid in decorative

patterns to make even the most pedestrian structure look exciting. Patterns can be

formed according to an array of traditional bonds, or created by inserting bricks of

various colors, or even made by including different materials such as tiles.

ABOVE **A simple but very decorative garden wall, with three courses set in a honeycomb pattern under a coping of soldier bricks.**

ABOVE (INSET) **A traditional English Sussex farmyard wall with the bricks set in a heading bond (the courses run at a diagonal angle to the ground).**

ABOVE Stark winter weather reveals the full decorative structure of these pergola pillars. It has been achieved by setting selected bricks slightly proud of the primary face, to create a subtle English diaper pattern (see page 28), and also by topping the pillars with chevron or zigzag headers, formed by setting a course of bricks to show a series of faces at angles of 45° to the general surface of the pillar.

Brick barbecue

This impressive structure beats other barbecues hollow in terms of attractiveness and practicality. There is a huge area for cooking, large work surfaces, a couple of handy shelves, and a hearth chimney for the smoke. It makes an eye-catching garden feature, and out of barbecue season, the work surfaces and shelves would be good for displaying plants (place containers on saucers to avoid marking the surfaces).

TIME

Five days (assuming there is an existing footing).

SAFETY

Do not leave a lit barbecue unattended, especially if you have young children and pets.

YOU WILL NEED

Materials *for a barbecue 5.3 ft. high, 5.2 ft. wide, and 33 in. deep*
- Bricks: 377
- Concrete slabs: 4 slabs, 18 in. square and 1 in. thick
- Tiles: 30 tiles, 6 in. square and ¼ in. thick
- Slate: 6 random, fairly oval pieces, about 2 in. in diameter and ¼ in. thick
- Mortar: 1 part (88 lb.) portland cement and 4 parts (352 lb.) sand
- Wood: 9 pieces, 7.5 in. long, 1 in. wide, and 1 in. thick (sticks for center of former); 1 piece, 18 in. long, 1 in. wide, and 1 in. thick (trammel former); 1 piece, 5.6 ft. long, 1 in. wide, and 1 in. thick (long rule)
- Plywood: 2 pieces, 28 in. long, 14 in. wide, and 0.2 in. thick (former)
- Nails: 18 x 1 in.
- Grill kit: between 25–27 in. x 14–17 in.

Tools
- Tape measure, long rule, and piece of chalk
- Spade, fork, and shovel
- Wheelbarrow and bucket
- Sledgehammer
- Shovel and mixing board, or cement mixer
- Mason's trowel and pointing trowel
- Brick hammer and stonemason's hammer
- Brick chisel
- Rubber mallet
- Level
- Handsaw
- Jigsaw
- Claw hammer

EATING OUT

Everyone enjoys a barbecue—there is something very appealing about cooking and eating food outdoors in warm weather. This barbecue is ideal if you do a lot of entertaining, because it is bigger than average and built to last. It will banish forever those barbecuing balancing acts with tiny, feeble contraptions that seem to rust as you look at them.

Take considerable care when deciding on a location for the barbecue. It is obviously not feasible to move the completed structure, so before committing to a spot, have a trial cooking session there on a disposable barbecue. Watch out for hazards such as low branches, or plants growing on a pergola overhead that might shrivel in the heat or catch fire, and drawbacks such as being just too far away from the seating area. The barbecue needs a firm footing, so check what is under your existing patio (see page 21) or build a new footing as shown on page 110.

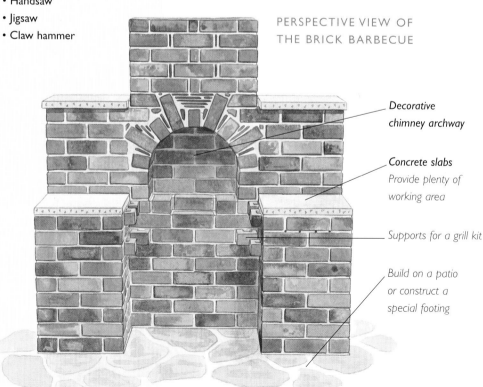

PERSPECTIVE VIEW OF THE BRICK BARBECUE

Decorative chimney archway

Concrete slabs
Provide plenty of working area

Supports for a grill kit

Build on a patio or construct a special footing

Brick barbecue

PLAN VIEW SHOWING THE LAYOUT OF THE FIRST COURSE OF BRICKS

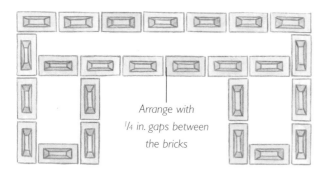

Arrange with ¼ in. gaps between the bricks

PLAN VIEW SHOWING THE LAYOUT OF THE SECOND COURSE OF BRICKS

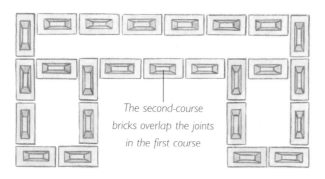

The second-course bricks overlap the joints in the first course

PLAN VIEW SHOWING THE LAYOUT OF THE SEVENTH COURSE OF BRICKS

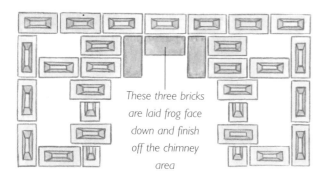

These three bricks are laid frog face down and finish off the chimney area

PLAN VIEW SHOWING THE LAYOUT OF THE NINTH COURSE OF BRICKS

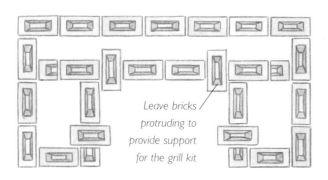

Leave bricks protruding to provide support for the grill kit

FRONT VIEW OF THE ARCH FORMER (ONE SIDE REMOVED)

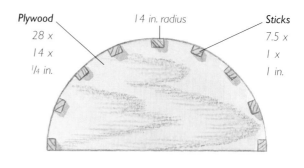

Plywood
28 x
14 x
¼ in.

14 in. radius

Sticks
7.5 x
1 x
1 in.

PERSPECTIVE VIEW OF THE ARCH FORMER

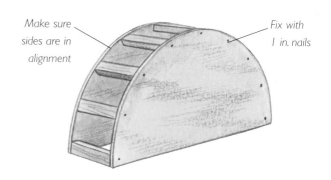

Make sure sides are in alignment

Fix with 1 in. nails

SIDE VIEW OF THE BRICK BARBECUE

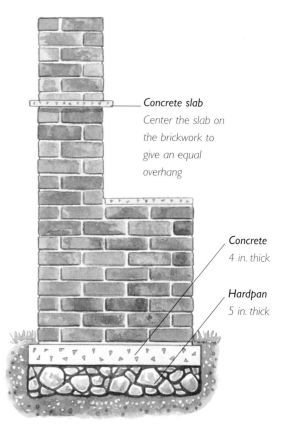

Concrete slab
Center the slab on the brickwork to give an equal overhang

Concrete
4 in. thick

Hardpan
5 in. thick

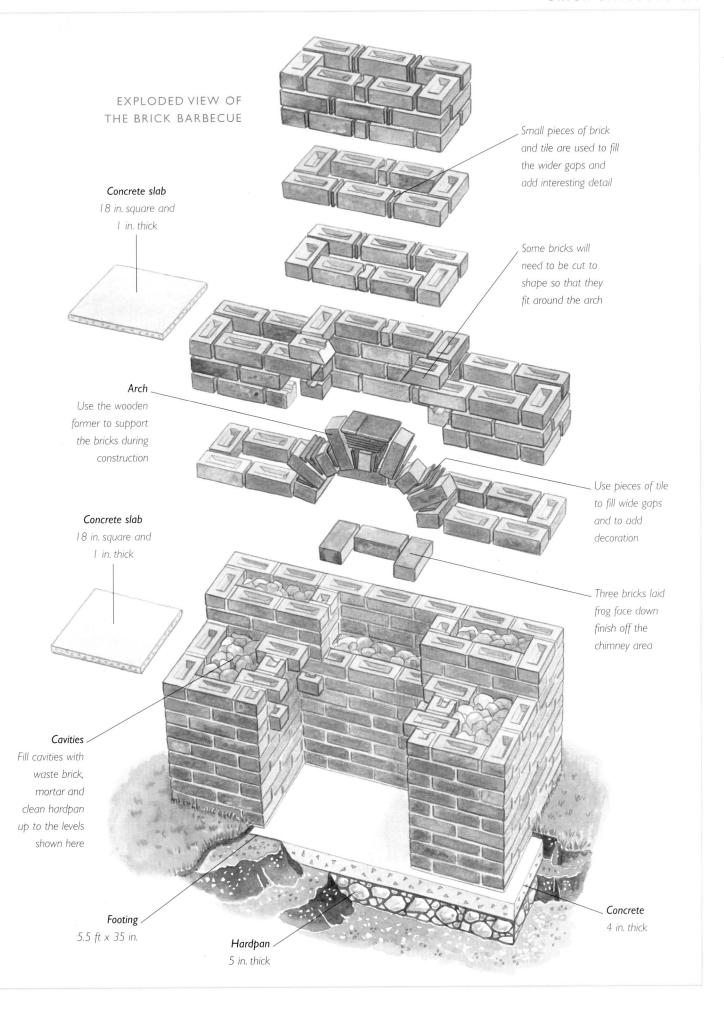

EXPLODED VIEW OF
THE BRICK BARBECUE

Small pieces of brick
and tile are used to fill
the wider gaps and
add interesting detail

Concrete slab
18 in. square and
1 in. thick

Some bricks will
need to be cut to
shape so that they
fit around the arch

Arch
Use the wooden
former to support
the bricks during
construction

Use pieces of tile
to fill wide gaps
and to add
decoration

Concrete slab
18 in. square and
1 in. thick

Three bricks laid
frog face down
finish off the
chimney area

Cavities
Fill cavities with
waste brick,
mortar and
clean hardpan
up to the levels
shown here

Concrete
4 in. thick

Footing
5.5 ft x 35 in.

Hardpan
5 in. thick

Step-by-step: **Making the brick barbecue**

First course
Spend time perfecting
the layout

Mortar
Use a fairly stiff mortar
for the first course

Guidelines
Draw around
the layout
with chalk

Squareness
It is vital that
the angles
are at 90°

Leveling
Make
adjustments to
ensure that the
bricks are level

1 If you do not have an existing patio area that provides a firm footing on which to build, dig a 9in.-deep hole and lay 5 in. of compacted hardpan and 4 in. of concrete (add 2 in. to the depth of the hole if the barbecue will be surrounded by grass—this lets the bricks merge into the grass). Mark out the outer area of the barbecue and practice arranging your first course of bricks (without mortar) in the order shown. Check that the grill and tray fit.

2 If you are working on an existing patio, check that it is level in all directions before proceeding. If it does slope, it can probably be compensated for by adding extra mortar in the first course. If the slope is too great (more than $1/4$ in. across the length of the barbecue), you will need to cast a level concrete slab on top, at least $1\frac{1}{2}$ in. thick. Begin laying the first course of bricks.

Waste
All the brick and mortar waste
can be put into the cavities

Corners
As you build
the corners,
check that they
are true with
the level

Supports
Center the
support bricks
across the
thickness of
the wall

Levels
Ensure the
support bricks
are level with
each other

3 Continue building up the walls, making sure all the joints are staggered and that the structure is level and vertical. Check each brick with the level before proceeding to the next, and take time to finish off the joints between bricks before the mortar dries.

4 Complete six courses, and on the seventh course change the layout of bricks as shown, so that four bricks stick out into the recess. The ends of these bricks provide support for the metal tray.

Grill
The grill will finish up two
courses higher than the tray

Arch
Use mortar and slate to correct
the angle of bricks around the arch

Levels
Make
adjustments to
ensure the grill
and tray are
level and
parallel with
each other

Supports
Use thin bits
of wood or
slate to level
the former

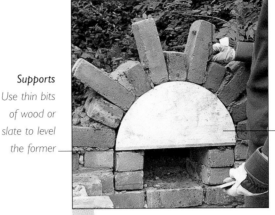

Former
Propped up
on bricks

5 Continue building upward and incorporate support for the grill in the ninth course. Check that both the tray and grill fit in the recess, and then put them aside. At this stage, the brickwork either side of the recess is complete and you can now concentrate on the back of the barbecue. Make a wooden former to support the brickwork arch as in the Tudor Arch Wall Niche project on pages 94–99.

6 Prop up the former on bricks. Build the arch over it, using pieces of slate to help prop up the bricks over the arch. Starting from one side, put mortar on the bricks that are already there, then place one of the arch bricks, making sure it is pointing to the center of the arch (if not, push a piece of slate underneath to prop it to the correct angle). Continue laying bricks around the arch, and when you are almost at the center, start at the other side. Finish by inserting a central brick.

Courses
Make sure the bricks are
level each side of the arch

Tiles
Use broken
tiles to make
decorative infills

Levels
Make repeated
checks with the
level

Worktops
Use mortar
and slate to
level the slabs

7 Fill the cavities in the barbecue, up to the the level of the grill, with waste brick, mortar, and clean hardpan. Fill in the area over the arch with bricks cut to size and pieces of decorative tile. Use the pointing trowel to fill any gaps and tidy up the mortar joints as you build.

8 Complete building the chimney stack, checking levels as you work. Check the concrete slab surfaces fit and bed them level on a $1/4$ in.-thick layer of mortar. Finish off all the mortar joints. Wait a few days before having a barbecue, or the heat will dry out the mortar too quickly.

Feature wall

An ancient brick wall is a unique piece of history, as well as a charming structure. It is a record of changing needs—as time passes, doors and windows are altered and filled in with bits of this and that. This project aims to achieve a similar patchwork of interesting features. If you wish, you can make it as a piece of art that reflects your own personal history, with structures and textures to represent significant events in your own life, such as marriage or the birth of a child.

TIME

Six days (do not lay more than four courses in a day).

SAFETY

Add a buttress behind the wall to make it safer if you have children (see page 29).

YOU WILL NEED

Materials *for a wall 5.6 ft. high and 8.5 ft. long*
- Bricks: 306
- Stone: 1 slab, 17 in. long, 10 in. wide, and 2.5 in. thick; 2 boulders, 8 in. in diameter; 14 small pieces, 12 in. long, 8 in. wide, and 1 in. thick
- Millstone: 16 in. in diameter and 4 in. thick
- Tiles: 9 tiles, 8.5 in. long, 6 in. wide, and ½ in. thick
- Cobblestones: 40 cobble-stones, 2 in. in diameter
- Pebbles: 150 pebbles, ½ in. in diameter
- Hardpan: 7 cu. feet
- Concrete: 1 part (132 lb.) portland cement and 4 parts (528 lb.) ballast
- Mortar: 1 part (132 lb.) portland cement and 4 parts (528 lb.) sand
- Wood: 8 pieces, 8 in. long, 1 in. wide, and 1 in. thick (sticks for center of former); 1 piece, 22 in. long, 1 in. wide, and 1 in. thick (trammel former)

- Plywood: 2 pieces, 18 in. long, 15 in. wide, and ¼ in. thick (former)
- Nails: 16 x 1.5 in.

Tools
- Tape measure, pegs, string, long rule, and a piece of chalk
- Spade and fork
- Wheelbarrow and bucket
- Sledgehammer
- Shovel and mixing board, or cement mixer
- Mason's trowel and pointing trowel
- Brick hammer and stonemason's hammer
- Brick chisel
- Level
- Handsaw
- Jigsaw
- Claw hammer

PLAN VIEW SHOWING THE FIRST COURSE OF BRICKS

Footing
8.7 ft. x 12 in.

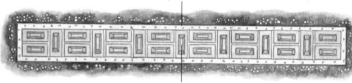

Two-brick-thick wall
Laid in a Flemish bond

PLAN VIEW SHOWING THE SECOND COURSE OF BRICKS

In the second course, the bricks are laid so that they overlap the joints in the first course

TIME AND TEXTURE

There is something fascinating about walking through the ruins of a once-magnificent castle or abbey, and seeing crumbling archways held up as if by magic, and staircases that lead nowhere. Wouldn't it be great to have your own mysterious ruin at the bottom of the garden? Well, now is your chance to build something unusual with a historical feel.

This wall is 5.6 ft. high, and so needs a strong footing as illustrated on page 116. We haven't built reinforcing piers or buttresses, because the wall is at the bottom of the garden beside a hedge and is unlikely to be disturbed, but if you have children who are likely to play nearby, you must include extra support (see Supporting Piers and Buttresses on page 29).

All sorts of brick and stone materials can be built into this wall, so don't feel that you have to follow the drawings exactly. Pieces of carved stone, fossils, or even shells would also look great bedded in the mortar.

Feature wall

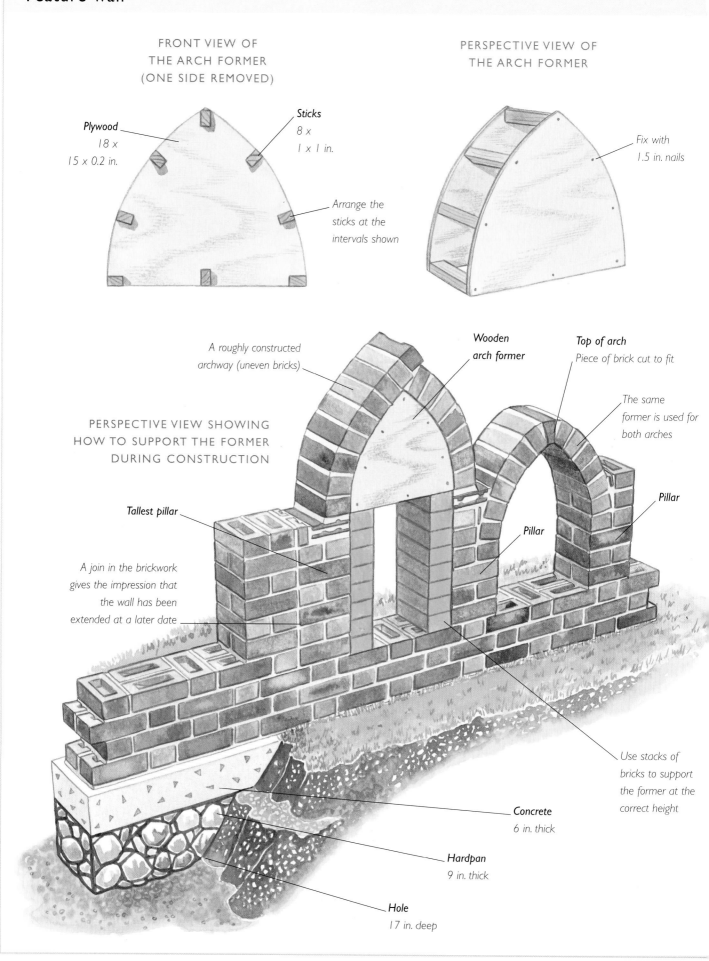

FRONT VIEW OF
THE ARCH FORMER
(ONE SIDE REMOVED)

Plywood
18 x
15 x 0.2 in.

Sticks
8 x
1 x 1 in.

Arrange the
sticks at the
intervals shown

PERSPECTIVE VIEW OF
THE ARCH FORMER

Fix with
1.5 in. nails

A roughly constructed
archway (uneven bricks)

Wooden
arch former

Top of arch
Piece of brick cut to fit

The same
former is used for
both arches

PERSPECTIVE VIEW SHOWING
HOW TO SUPPORT THE FORMER
DURING CONSTRUCTION

Tallest pillar

A join in the brickwork
gives the impression that
the wall has been
extended at a later date

Pillar

Pillar

Use stacks of
bricks to support
the former at the
correct height

Concrete
6 in. thick

Hardpan
9 in. thick

Hole
17 in. deep

EXPLODED VIEW OF THE FEATURE WALL

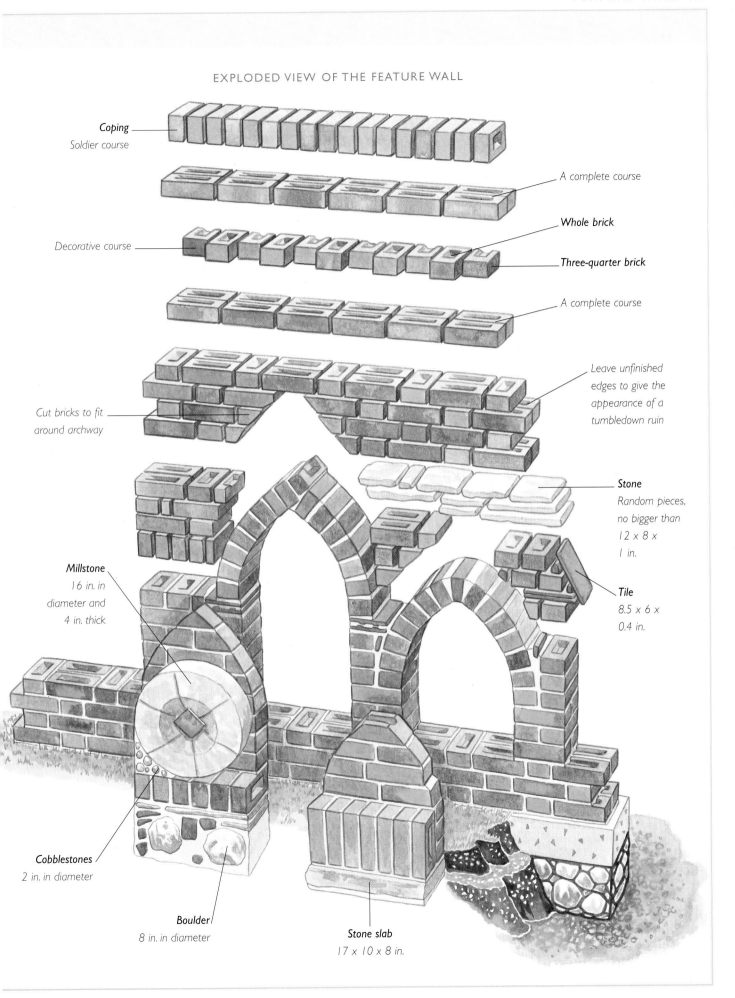

Coping
Soldier course

A complete course

Whole brick

Decorative course

Three-quarter brick

A complete course

Cut bricks to fit around archway

Leave unfinished edges to give the appearance of a tumbledown ruin

Stone
Random pieces, no bigger than 12 x 8 x 1 in.

Tile
8.5 x 6 x 0.4 in.

Millstone
16 in. in diameter and 4 in. thick

Cobblestones
2 in. in diameter

Boulder
8 in. in diameter

Stone slab
17 x 10 x 8 in.

Step-by-step: **Making the feature wall**

Bond
Use a Flemish bond to build the wall three courses high

Level
Ensure the pillars are upright and parallel

Levels
Ensure the pillars are level with each other

Levels
Use the level to check the levels

Pillar
Build two, two-by-two brick pillars

1 Dig a footing hole 17 in. deep, and lay 9 in. of compacted hardpan and 6 in. of concrete. Use chalk and a string line or long rule to mark the position of the wall. Build three courses of bricks in the decorative bond shown. Make sure all the vertical joints are staggered and check that the wall is level and vertical. The finished wall is meant to look like an old structure that has been repaired many times over the years, so just finish the joints by scraping out excess mortar and don't bother filling gaps.

2 Build up two brick pillars (as shown here) and a third, taller pillar (as shown in the drawings on pages 116–117). Make sure all the bricks are turned so that they overlap the joints of the bricks below and check that they are level using the level.

Top of arch
Use a piece of brick cut to fit

Former
Refer to the working drawings for the shape of the former

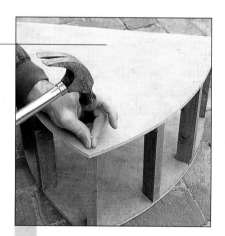

Soldier bricks
Lay bricks on their stretcher face over the former

Former
Propped up on bricks

3 Make a wooden former to support the brickwork arch. You can draw the shape of the arch on the plywood using a trammel former (see page 27) to make the two 18 in.-radius arcs. Cut out the arch shape with the jigsaw. Join the pieces together as shown in the Tudor Arch Wall Niche project on pages 94–99.

4 Prop up the wooden former on piles of bricks between the two small pillars. Lay bricks up each side of the arch, leaving equal spaces between each brick and tapping them down with the handle of the brick hammer. At the top of the arch, lay a brick that has been cut to fit.

Stepped detail
*Use tiles to build
idiosyncratic details*

Top of arch
Bricks cut to fit

Bond
*Continue the
Flemish bond
over the arch*

Infill
*Fill the
recess with
found items*

Detailing
*Complete the
recess by filling
in around the
millstone with
mortar and
cobbles*

5 Build around the arch with brick and pieces of tile and stone as shown in the drawing (or according to your own design). This is a good way of using up spare bricks and stone. When the mortar has dried, remove the wooden former and reuse it to build the second (higher) arch. Fill in the lower arch with bricks and stone. Brick up the back of the higher arch, using a single thickness of bricks.

6 Mortar the millstone in the recess of the higher arch and fill in around it with cobblestones and mortar. Interesting salvaged architectural features or broken pieces of crockery could also be incorporated into the structure.

7 Finish building the regular courses above the level of the arches and start on the decorative strips of bricks at the top. Cut bricks in half and use these for the recessed details. Complete the building process with a course of soldier bricks to form the coping.

Soldier bricks
*Top the wall
with a coping
of soldier bricks*

Helpful hint

You can make brickwork look old and weathered by scraping mortar from between the bricks, and then using a wire brush to erode the mortar before it dries completely.

Waterspout

A small yard or a quiet corner of the garden can be magically enhanced by the addition of a waterspout. A gentle stream of water spouts through a mask, set into a brick wall topped by an arch, and splashes onto a couple of splash tiles protruding from the wall before tumbling into a reservoir pool. If you enjoy the therapeutic sight and sound of falling water, this striking project will make an exciting feature.

YOU WILL NEED

Materials *for a wall, waterspout, and reservoir 4.8 ft. high, 37 in. wide, and 32 in. deep*

- Bricks: 205
- Tiles: 24 tiles, 9.5 in. long, 6 in. wide, and ½ in. thick
- Mortar: 1 part (55 lb.) portland cement and 4 parts (220 lb.) sand
- Render: 1 part (55 lb.) portland cement and 4 parts (220 lb.) sharp sand
- Wood: 10 pieces, 8 in. long, 1 in. wide, and 1 in. thick (sticks for center of former); 1 piece, 18 in. long, 1 in. wide, and 1 in. thick (trammel former)
- Plywood: 2 pieces, 27 in. long, 14 in. wide, and ¼ in. thick (former)
- Nails: 20 x 1.5 in.
- Armored plastic cable: 13 ft. x 2 in. in diameter (to protect electric cable and water supply pipe)
- Flexible plastic cable (water supply pipe): 6.5 ft. (to fit on pump and run through armored cable 2 in. in diameter)
- Small submersible pump
- Mask: 8–12 in. high
- Tank sealer: 3½ fl oz.

Tools
- Tape measure, long rule, and piece of chalk
- Hacksaw to cut pipe
- Wheelbarrow and bucket
- Shovel and mixing board, or cement mixer
- Mason's trowel and pointing trowel
- Brick hammer and stonemason's hammer
- Brick chisel
- Level
- Handsaw
- Jigsaw
- Claw hammer

WATER SETS THE MOOD

Fountains, waterfalls, cascades, and waterspouts all make great garden or yard features—the sight and sound of water trickling or splashing into a pool below is mesmerising and relaxing. The waterspout is a fairly traditional feature in formal, classical gardens, but is also perfect for modern gardens of all descriptions.

This design has the advantage of being freestanding, but most waterspout designs rely on fixing a mask to an existing wall, which entails installing cablework within the wall for the water and power supplies, and this is quite an engineering job. With this project, you don't need an existing wall (but you can build it in front of a wall) and the cablework is concealed within a cavity at the back of the structure.

You may like to consider variations in the overall shape of the structure (perhaps smaller, or squared off at the top), or add decoration such as ornate tile details. You may prefer a different type of wall mask: we have chosen a strong character, but you could have something more restrained like a lion's head, or even design and make something of your own in clay or copper.

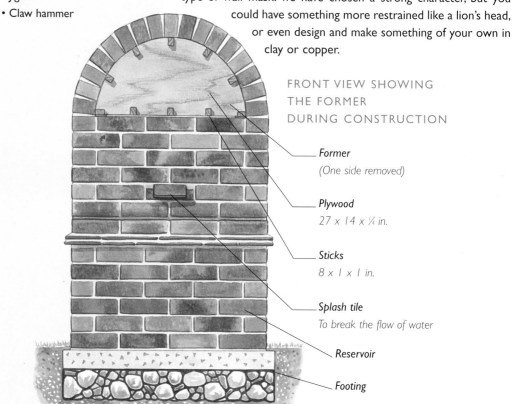

FRONT VIEW SHOWING THE FORMER DURING CONSTRUCTION

Former
(One side removed)

Plywood
27 x 14 x ¼ in.

Sticks
8 x 1 x 1 in.

Splash tile
To break the flow of water

Reservoir

Footing

Waterspout

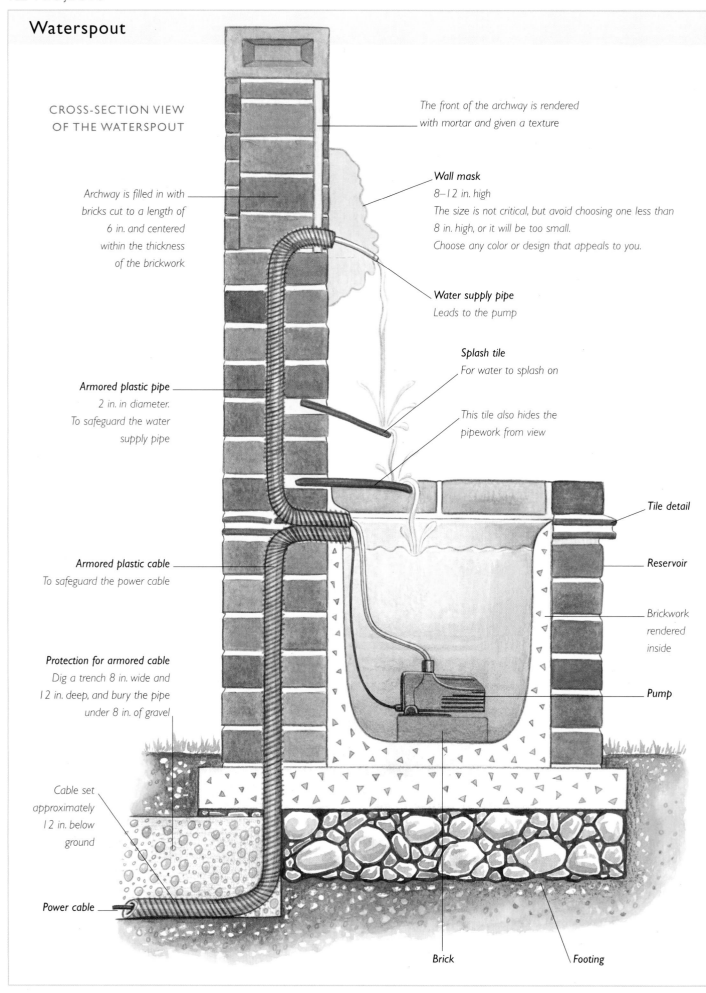

CROSS-SECTION VIEW
OF THE WATERSPOUT

Archway is filled in with bricks cut to a length of 6 in. and centered within the thickness of the brickwork

The front of the archway is rendered with mortar and given a texture

Wall mask
8–12 in. high
The size is not critical, but avoid choosing one less than 8 in. high, or it will be too small. Choose any color or design that appeals to you.

Water supply pipe
Leads to the pump

Splash tile
For water to splash on

This tile also hides the pipework from view

Armored plastic pipe
2 in. in diameter. To safeguard the water supply pipe

Tile detail

Reservoir

Armored plastic cable
To safeguard the power cable

Brickwork rendered inside

Pump

Protection for armored cable
Dig a trench 8 in. wide and 12 in. deep, and bury the pipe under 8 in. of gravel

Cable set approximately 12 in. below ground

Power cable

Brick

Footing

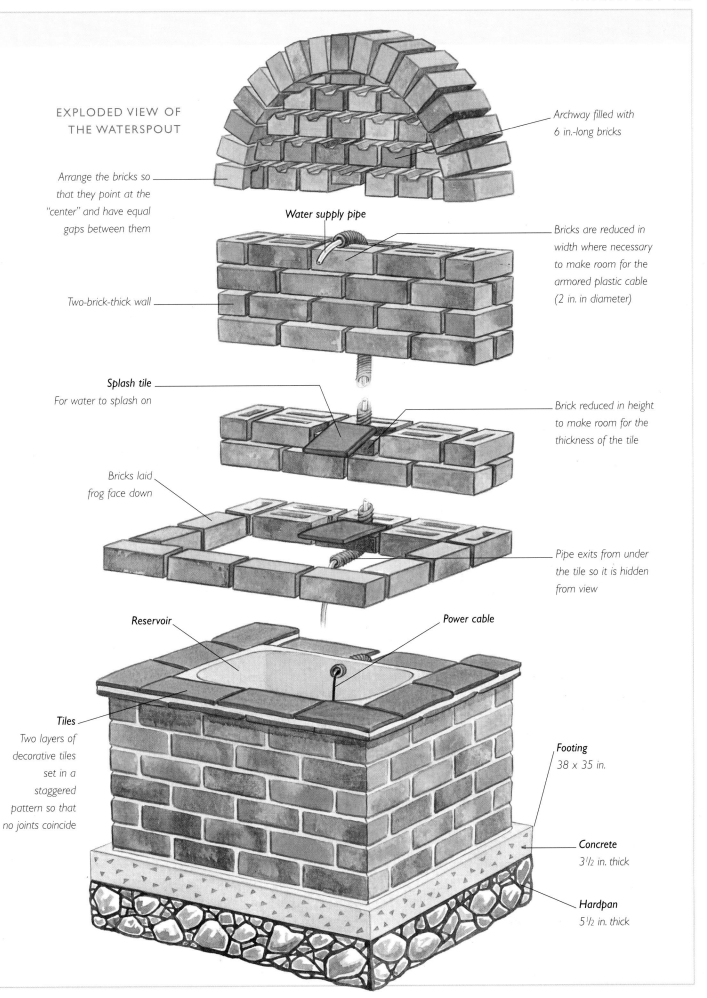

EXPLODED VIEW OF
THE WATERSPOUT

*Arrange the bricks so
that they point at the
"center" and have equal
gaps between them*

Archway filled with
6 in.-long bricks

Water supply pipe

Bricks are reduced in
*width where necessary
to make room for the
armored plastic cable
(2 in. in diameter)*

Two-brick-thick wall

Splash tile
For water to splash on

Brick reduced in height
*to make room for the
thickness of the tile*

*Bricks laid
frog face down*

Pipe exits from under
*the tile so it is hidden
from view*

Reservoir

Power cable

Tiles
*Two layers of
decorative tiles
set in a
staggered
pattern so that
no joints coincide*

Footing
38 x 35 in.

Concrete
3½ in. thick

Hardpan
5½ in. thick

Step-by-step: **Making the waterspout**

Back wall
Incorporate a second wall at the back of the box

Pipes
Build in two armoured pipes— one for water and one for power

Bond
Build the wall using a stretcher bond

Courses
After every few courses, scrape off excess mortar and tidy up the joints between the bricks

Coping tiles
Top the wall with a double-tile coping

1 Find a firm area of patio to build on (with a suitable footing—see page 21), or construct a level footing using 5½ in. of compacted hardpan and 3½ in. of concrete. Mark out the area of the brickwork. Build the reservoir: a simple box shape that incorporates a second wall at the back for housing the pipes. Cut bricks to fit around the armored cable containing the electric cable.

2 Continue building until you have completed six courses. Lay two courses of tiles on ¼ in.-thick mortar. Overlap the joints as shown, and avoid cutting them if possible. If the tiles are curved, lay them so the bottom layer curves upward and the top layer curves downward. Position the armored cable for the water supply pipe.

Splash tile
The distance the tiles protrude, and their angle, affect the way the water falls. Experiment with tiles propped up in position under the mask before starting construction. Pour water through the mask to ascertain how the tiles should be placed for best effect. Take measurements from this mock-up

3 To top the reservoir, lay a line of bricks (frog side down) around the box shape. Finish the joint between the bricks and the tiles with an angled mortar detail. Fix a splash tile into the back wall. Continue building the back wall, cutting bricks where necessary to fit around the water supply pipe. Refer to the drawings to see how the bricks are laid for best effect.

Helpful hint

Some of the bricks around the cable require cutting lengthwise, but for the rest it is enough just to break off the corner with a hammer.

Former
Plywood or other
waste wood

Trammel former
Use the
trammel former
to draw
semicircles with
a radius
of 14 in.

Arch
Run bricks around the arch, laying
them on their stretcher face

Former
Prop up
the former
on wedges
of wood

Arch bricks
Use a bit of
waste tile to
space the
arch bricks

4 Complete building the back wall, incorporating a second splash tile and finishing with the water supply pipe sticking out of the center of the cavity. Make a wooden former for the arch shape: mark semicircles with a 14 in. radius on the plywood using a trammel former (see page 27). Cut out with the jigsaw. Join the pieces together as described in the Tudor Arch Wall Niche project on pages 94–99.

5 Place the former on small scraps of wood and practice placing bricks (on their stretcher face) around the curve. When you are confident and ready to start, lay each brick on a generous angled bed of mortar, and tap it down into position. If you need to make major corrections, it is better to start again with fresh mortar. Remove the former by pulling out the scraps of wood beneath.

Pipe
As you render
around the
pipe, make
sure that it
doesn't slip
back into
the wall

6 Brick up the back of the wall under the arch with bricks that have been reduced in length and laid with the header faces (ends) facing forward. Leave the water supply pipe poking out at the front, level with the bottom of the arch. Render the arch recess and texture it with a piece of wood. Render the inside of the reservoir pool with mortar made with sharp sand, then leave to dry and coat with tank sealer. After a few days, fit the mask and install the pump.

Rendering
Cover the recessed
arch with mortar
and create a
grooved texture
with a piece of
waste wood

Glossary

Backfilling To fill or pack a cavity (behind a wall or in a footing trench hole) with earth in order to bring the ground up to the desired level.

Bedding The process of pressing a brick, slab, or stone into a bed or layer of wet mortar and ensuring that it is level.

Buttering The act of using a trowel during bricklaying to cover some part of a brick with wet mortar, prior to setting it in position on a bed of mortar.

Compacting Using a sledgehammer or the weight of the body to press down a layer of sand, earth, or hardpan.

Coursing Part of the process of bricklaying—bedding a number of bricks on a bed of mortar in order to build a course (a horizontal layer of bricks).

Curing time The time taken for mortar or concrete to become firm and stable. "Part-cured" means that the mortar or concrete is firm enough to bear a small amount of weight.

Floating The procedure of using a metal, plastic, or wooden float to skim wet concrete or mortar to a smooth and level finish.

Leveling Using a level to decide whether or not a structure or brick is level (horizontally parallel to the ground, or vertically at right angles to the ground), and then making adjustments to bring individual bricks into line.

Marking out Using string, pegs and a tape measure to variously set out the area of a footing on the ground. Also to mark an individual brick in readiness for cutting.

Pecking Using the edge of a large trowel or the chisel end of a brick hammer to nibble the ragged edge of a part-cut brick back to a marked line.

Planning The procedure of considering a project, viewing the site, making drawings, working out quantities and costs, prior to starting work. Thorough planning is vital in order to avoid hold-ups and the wastage of materials.

Pointing Using a trowel, stick, or a tool of your choice to bring mortar joints to the desired finish.

Raking out Using a trowel to rake out some part of the mortar from between courses, so that the edges of the bricks are clearly and crisply revealed.

Sighting To judge by eye whether or not a cut, joint, or structure is level or true. To look down or along a wall in order to determine whether or not the structure is level.

Siting Deciding whereabouts on the site—in the garden or on the plot—the structure is going to be placed. The aspect, sun, shade, and proximity to the house may need to be taken into consideration.

Sourcing Questioning suppliers by phone, e-mail, or letter, in order to make decisions concerning the best source for materials—especially sand, cement, and bricks.

Tamping The act of using a length of wood to compact and level wet concrete.

Trial run or dry run Setting out the components of a structure, without using concrete or mortar, in order to ascertain whether or not the pattern of bricks is going to work out.

Trimming Using a hammer or the edge of a large trowel to cut and sculpt a brick to a good finish.

Watering Wetting bricks at the start of a work session, prior to bedding them on mortar.

Wire brushing Using a wire-bristle brush to remove dry mortar from the face of bricks—for example, on a wall or the surface of a path or patio.

Suppliers

UK

Bricks, concrete, cement

Baggeridge Brick Plc
Fir Street
Sedgley
Dudley
West Midlands
DY3 4AA
Tel: (01902) 880555
Fax: (01902) 880432
www.baggeridge.co.uk
(Suppliers of bricks, pavers etc.)

Freshfield Lane Brickworks
Dane Hill
Haywards Heath
West Sussex
RH17 7HH
Tel: (01825) 790350
www.flb.uk.com

Heritage Reclaimed Brick Co.
Unit 2, 24 Willow Lane
Mitcham
Surrey
CR4 4NA
Tel: (020) 8687 1907

Ibstock Bricks Ltd
Ashdown Works
Turkey Road
Bexhill-on-Sea
East Sussex
TN39 5HY
Tel: (01424) 847400

The Brick Warehouse
18–22 Northdown Street
London
N1 9BG
Tel: (020) 7833 9992

York Handmade Brick
   Company Ltd
Winchester House
Forest Lane
Alne
York
YO61 1TU
Tel: (01347) 838881
Fax: (01347) 838885
www.yorkhandmade.co.uk
(Suppliers of handmade bricks, paving materials and special shapes)

**General do-it-yourself
suppliers
(branches nationwide)**

B & Q Plc
1 Hampshire Corporate Park
Chandlers Ford
Eastleigh
Hampshire
SO53 3YX
Tel: (01703) 256256

Focus Do-It-All Group Ltd
Gawsworth House
Westmere Drive
Crewe
Cheshire
CW1 6XB
Tel: (01384) 456456

Homebase Ltd
Beddington House
Railway Approach
Wallington
Surrey
SM6 0HB
Tel: (020) 8784 7200

Wickes
Wickes House
120–138 Station Road
Harrow
Middlesex
HA1 2QB
Tel: (0870) 6089001

SOUTH AFRICA

**Bricks, concrete, portland
cement**

Cement and Concrete Institute
Portland Park
Old Pretoria Road
Halfway House
Midrand 1685
Tel: (011) 315 0300

Clay Brick Association
PO Box 1284
Halfway House
Johannesburg 1685
Tel: (011) 805 4206

Natal Master Builders'
    Association Centre
40 Essex Terrace
Westville 3630
Tel: (031) 266 7070

The Building Centre
Belmont Square
Rondebosch
Cape Town 7700
Tel: (021) 685 3040

AUSTRALIA

ABC Timber & Building Supplies
46 Auburn Road
Regents Park
NSW 2143
Tel: (02) 9645 2511

BBC Hardware
Bld A
Cnr. Cambridge &
    Chester Streets
Epping
NSW 2121
Tel: (02) 9876 0888

Bowens Timber &
    Building Supplies
135–173 Macaulay Road
North Melbourne
VIC 3051
Tel: (03) 9328 1041

Bunnings Building Supplies
152 Pilbara Street
Welshpool
WA 6106
Tel: (08) 9365 1555

Elite Paving
33 Neilson Crescent
Bligh Park
NSW 2756
Tel: (4574 1414)

Pine Rivers Landscaping Supplies
93 South Pine Road
Strathpine
QLD 4500
Tel: (07) 3205 6708

Sydney Stone Yard
1/3A Stanley Road
Randwick
NSW 2031
Tel: (02) 9326 4479

NEW ZEALAND

Firth Industries
Freephone: 0800 800 576

Placemakers
Freephone: 0800 425 2269

Stevenson Building Supplies
Freephone: 0800 610 710
(Blocks, bricks, paving, concrete)

Southtile
654 North Road
Invercargill
Tel: (03) 215 9179
Freephone: 0800 768 848
(Tiles and bricks)

ITM Building Centres
Freephone: 0800 367 486

Index